NEW PARADIGM

COOKING

A TASTEFUL SHIFT IN HEALTHY EATING

NEW PARADIGM
COOKING

™

NANCY E. SANDBACH,
MS, RD, LDN

FRANK A. TERRANOVA,
CCE, CEC

BRADLEY J. WARE,
M.Ed, CCC, CCE

Recipe for cover photograph, Thai Noodle Salad, is on page 33.
Recipe for cover photograph, Breast of Chicken Cacciatore Contemporary-Style, is on page 63.
Recipe for cover photograph, Strawberry Yogurt Mousse with Grand Marnier Sauce, is on page 150.

Published by Paradigm Cooking, Inc.

Copyright© Paradigm Cooking, Inc.
P.O. Box 3641
Cranston, Rhode Island 02910

Library of Congress Number: 96-84940
ISBN: 0-9652360-0-5

Edited, Designed, and Manufactured by
Favorite Recipes® Press
P.O. Box 305142
Nashville, Tennessee 37230
1-800-358-0560
Managing Editor: Mary Cummings
Project Manager: Debbie Van Mol
Cover and Book Design: Brad Whitfield
Typographer: Sara Anglin

Manufactured in the United States
First Printing: 1996   10,000 copies

Acknowledgements

We would like to thank the following companies for their assistance in the development of this book:

Frederick Wildman & Sons, Ltd.
307 East 53rd Street
New York, New York 10022
1-800-Red Wine

The Gourmet Outlet
2301 Purchase Street
New Bedford, Massachussetts
1-800-249-0447

Yum, Inc.
Food Styling and Photography
P.O. Box 9116
Pawtucket, Rhode Island 02862
401-822-0815

Foreword

In response to a more educated consumer, chefs are increasingly asked to produce nutritious food that can still excite the palate. The challenge is to reduce or even eliminate dietary excesses such as fat, sodium, and cholesterol. *New Paradigm Cooking* offers the food enthusiast—from the novice cook to the professional chef—an opportunity to think in a new way when it comes to cooking and to change their cooking habits, the end result being healthier, even more delicious recipes. If this book has one message, it is: You do not have to sacrifice taste.

Having known the three individuals who wrote this book, I am confident that with their educational backgrounds and professional accomplishments they have created a book that can be used by all levels of home cooks and professional chefs. I personally enjoy the simplicity of the recipes in this book and, more importantly, the complexity of taste many of these dishes have to offer. I trust you will as well.

The basic objectives we teach at Johnson & Wales University include the relationship between nutrient intake and good health, food fundamentals and their effect on lifestyles and cultures, and the ability to recognize foods and eating habits that are essential to proper nutrition. It is crucial that our students gain a broad understanding of nutrition so that prudent menu decisions can be made when they graduate and become chefs.

Good nutrition is not just another trend. It is here to stay, and it works, as clearly evidenced in *New Paradigm Cooking*.

Thomas L. Wright
Vice President of Culinary Education
Johnson & Wales University

Contents

Introduction

What is a paradigm (`para-dime') and what is *New Paradigm Cooking?*

Paradigm means pattern or model. You can think of a paradigm as a set of rules which you follow in order to get something accomplished. Generally, we follow paradigms without question. For instance, in the United States a common paradigm is that formal schooling takes place between the months of September and June. That's just the way it always has been done.

Related to food preparation, the current paradigm seems to go two ways. Either recipes are not in tune with today's more health-conscious diner or, if they are, the recipes are less food than we'd like. Ingredients are bland and seldom is a high-fat food to be found. This too is just the way it has always been done.

It's time for *New Paradigm Cooking.* Let's change the rules! Just because we're used to the extremes of decadent high-fat meals or spartan low-fat offerings doesn't mean that there is no in-between. It is possible to have cream in a low-fat entrée! Yes, you can leave the table feeling full and still have a healthy meal!

The recipes that follow observe the guidelines of the Food Guide Pyramid. You may have even noticed that in our logo we've turned the pyramid upside down and inserted a chef's hat. A visual reminder of the marriage that should exist between nutrient-abundant grains, fruits, and vegetables, protein-rich ingredients, dairy foods, and the culinary side of life—that together make a healthy diet both possible and enjoyable.

Perhaps you have not yet ventured into the world of healthful cooking and eating or you may not have been successful with adapting some of your favorite recipes. Relax . . . follow us! The recipes that follow bring together taste and health with some innovative twists.

The recipes in this book have been created, recreated, discussed, debated, analyzed, and enjoyed by two chefs and a registered dietitian. We hope that you will feel our efforts were worthwhile.

Guiding us along the way were a few basic principles:

▼ All foods in a low-fat healthy diet do not have to be low-fat.

You will notice as you look through these recipes that we have used items such as heavy cream, oils, and butter whenever we thought we could maintain the nutritional integrity of a dish. Sometimes, we even added oil! Some may gasp at the mere thought. We simply refused to have flavor take a back seat to nutrition. Taste must walk side by side with nutrition or not at all.

▼ There is more to healthy eating than just food.

Each recipe was carefully thought out so that how it is presented is visually, tastefully, and aromatically pleasing. In addition, a wine is suggested for each entrée recipe as wine serves to accent a meal as well.

▼ Great healthful meals cannot always be prepared in thirty minutes or less.

There are times when speed of meal preparation is paramount, and times when you have all afternoon to prepare a gustatory adventure. Know your situation and pick your recipes accordingly.

▼ Rules can be broken!

Remember . . . this is *New Paradigm Cooking!* If you don't have an ingredient or you have an urge to make an alteration, do it! And remember . . . sometimes what may be impossible with one paradigm (your old way of cooking) may be possible with another!

The appetizers presented here are unique. The paradigm of chips, dips, and "the usual" hot hors d'oeuvre has been shifted to include delights designed around the flavors of the Orient, Southwest, Italy, and the sea. Tantalize your taste buds with Thai-Style Turkey Lettuce Rolls, Black Bean Quesadillas with Tomato Cilantro Salsa, Roasted Pepper and Tomato Bruschetta, and Shrimp Cocktail with Gazpacho Sauce.

If canned soups are your soup-serving paradigm, change is possible with the freshly prepared varieties that follow. Chock-full of nutrients, soup can serve as an entrée when you are so inclined. Satisfy your appetite with Spicy Vegetable Cheese Chili, Creamy Seafood Corn Chowder, and Hearty Cabbage Soup with Dill Spaetzle. All soups are prepared with stocks for which recipes are provided in the appendix. If you choose to use canned broths just be aware that you will compromise on flavor, and the sodium content will soar, even when you use low-sodium types.

And who says a salad has to be just lettuce and tomatoes? You simply won't find anything so uninteresting here! Noodles, beans, seafood, and more work to create sensational salads that also can serve as meals. Experiment with Thai Noodle Salad, Tuscan Bean and Bread Salad, and Pan-Seared Shrimp Salad with Roasted Garlic Dressing, and no more will you refer to salad as "rabbit food."

A TASTEFUL SHIFT IN HEALTHY EATING

BEGINNINGS

™

APPETIZERS

SOUPS

SALADS

Black Bean Quesadillas
with Tomato Cilantro Salsa

Makes 4 servings

For the salsa

1/2 cup chopped red tomatoes
1/4 cup chopped scallions
2 tablespoons chopped fresh cilantro
1 garlic clove, chopped
1 tablespoon balsamic vinegar
1 teaspoon olive oil
1/2 teaspoon chili powder

For the quesadillas

1 cup cooked black beans
2 tablespoons chopped red onion
2 tablespoons chopped fresh basil
1 teaspoon chili powder
1 teaspoon minced jalapeño
1/2 teaspoon cumin
6 flour tortillas
1/4 cup shredded low-fat Vermont
   Cheddar cheese

To prepare the salsa
▼ Combine the tomatoes, scallions, cilantro and garlic in a bowl and mix well. Stir in a mixture of the balsamic vinegar, olive oil and chili powder.

To prepare the filling
▼ Preheat the oven to 450 degrees.
▼ Process the black beans, red onion, basil, chili powder, jalapeño and cumin in a food processor until puréed.

To assemble
▼ Spray a baking sheet with nonstick cooking spray. Arrange 4 of the tortillas in 2 stacks on the prepared baking sheet. Spread the top of each stack with the bean filling and sprinkle with the cheese. Top each stack with 1 tortilla.
▼ Bake for 4 to 6 minutes or until the tortillas are crisp. Cut each stack into quarters.
▼ Arrange the quesadillas on a heated serving platter and top with the salsa. Serve immediately.

Consider making tortillas, which are a staple in Mexican cuisine, a regular in your home. They are readily available in supermarkets and most of the ingredients required for these quesadillas are common to a cook's kitchen. Extremely versatile, one flour tortilla is nutritionally equivalent to two slices of bread and sets a new paradigm for sandwich eating.

Per Serving: Calories 279; Total Fat 6 g; Saturated Fat 1 g; Cholesterol 2 mg; Sodium 311 mg;
Carbohydrate 45 g; Fiber 7 g; Protein 11 g; Calcium 199 mg

Southwestern Pinto Bean Hummus

Makes 4 servings

2 cups cooked pinto beans, rinsed, drained
4 garlic cloves
1 tablespoon chili powder
1 tablespoon hot pepper sauce
1 tablespoon olive oil
$1/2$ teaspoon cumin
$1/2$ cup chopped scallions
2 tablespoons lime juice
1 tablespoon chopped fresh cilantro
Salt and pepper to taste
4 pita bread rounds

Method of preparation
▼ Preheat the oven to 400 degrees.
▼ Process the pinto beans, garlic, chili powder, hot pepper sauce, olive oil and cumin in a food processor until smooth. Add the scallions, lime juice, cilantro, salt and pepper.
▼ Process just until mixed. Chill, covered, in the refrigerator.
▼ Cut each pita bread round into halves. Cut each half into 2-inch pieces. Arrange on a nonstick baking sheet.
▼ Bake for 5 to 6 minutes or until crisp.
▼ Spoon the hummus into a serving bowl. Serve with the pita chips.

Traditional hummus is made with chick-peas and tahini or sesame seed paste. Hummus may be used as a spread or as a dip. This version utilizes pinto beans, a relative of the kidney bean, although they are speckled with red and beige colors. Typically used for refried beans, the pinto bean works nicely in this dip since it is complemented by the ususal "Mexican seasonings."

Per Serving: Calories 331; Total Fat 5 g; Saturated Fat 1 g; Cholesterol 0 mg; Sodium 346 mg; Carbohydrate 59 g; Fiber 10 g; Protein 13 g; Calcium 121 mg

Grilled Thai Eggplant

Makes 4 servings

1 pound Thai eggplant, sliced
2 tablespoons olive oil
2 tomatoes, peeled, seeded, chopped
2 tablespoons chopped fresh Thai basil
Salt and pepper to taste

Method of preparation

▼ Preheat the oven to 375 degrees. Spray a cold grill rack with nonstick cooking spray.
Preheat the grill.
▼ Brush both sides of the eggplant with some of the olive oil and place on the
prepared rack. Grill over hot coals for 1 minute on each side or until light brown.
Arrange the eggplant in a single layer on a baking sheet.
▼ Combine the remaining olive oil, tomatoes, basil, salt and pepper in a bowl and mix
well. Spoon over each eggplant slice.
▼ Bake for 10 minutes. Serve immediately.

Thai eggplant are unusual in contrast to the deep purple variety with which most people are familiar. Smaller in size, with a coloring of white and purple, the Thai varieties are found in most Asian supermarkets and gourmet specialty stores. The primary nutritional virtue of the eggplant is its fiber content.

Per Serving: Calories 108; Total Fat 7 g; Saturated Fat 1 g; Cholesterol 0 mg; Sodium 10 mg;
Carbohydrate 11 g; Fiber 4 g; Protein 2 g; Calcium 59 mg

Porcini Penne alla Fresca

Makes 4 servings

1³/₄ cups (¹/₄-inch pieces) red tomatoes
1³/₄ cups (¹/₄-inch pieces) yellow tomatoes
3 tablespoons garlic paste
2 tablespoons chopped fresh basil
2 tablespoons chopped fresh parsley
1 tablespoon extra-virgin olive oil
¹/₂ teaspoon red pepper flakes
Salt and black pepper to taste
12 ounces porcini penne

Method of preparation

▼ Combine the tomatoes, garlic paste, basil, parsley, olive oil, red pepper flakes, salt and black pepper in a bowl and mix well.
▼ Cook the pasta using package directions; drain.
▼ Combine the hot pasta and tomato mixture in a bowl and mix gently. Serve immediately.

"T" is for tomato, taste and a terrific source of vitamin C. All are illustrated in this recipe. Vital to the formation of connective tissue and for the healing of wounds, vitamin C may also help prevent the formation of cancer-causing substances. Since these tomatoes are not cooked, heat-sensitive vitamin C is preserved to a greater extent than in a cooked marinara sauce.

Per Serving: Calories 379; Total Fat 9 g; Saturated Fat 1 g; Cholesterol 0 mg; Sodium 38 mg; Carbohydrate 74 g; Fiber 2 g; Protein 12 g; Calcium 12 mg

Roasted Pepper and Tomato Bruschetta

Makes 4 servings

8 ounces yellow bell peppers
8 ounces green bell peppers
$1/2$ cup chopped red tomato
1 tablespoon olive oil
1 tablespoon chopped fresh basil
1 tablespoon chopped fresh parsley
1 garlic clove, minced
$1/2$ loaf Italian bread, sliced horizontally into halves
2 tablespoons grated Parmesan cheese

Method of preparation
▼ Preheat the oven to 400 degrees.
▼ Arrange the bell peppers stem side down on a nonstick baking sheet. Bake for 15 minutes or until brown. Place the bell peppers in a sealable plastic bag. Seal the bag.
▼ Let stand for 15 to 20 minutes or until the skins become tender. Peel and finely chop the bell peppers, discarding the skins and seeds. Combine the bell peppers, tomato, olive oil, basil, parsley and garlic in a bowl and mix well.
▼ Preheat the broiler.
▼ Arrange the bread cut side up on a baking sheet. Broil until brown. Spread with the bell pepper mixture and sprinkle with the cheese.
▼ Broil until light brown; cut into slices. Arrange the bruschetta on a heated serving platter. Serve immediately.

Peppers come in many shapes and sizes and really have nothing in common with black pepper seasoning, except for the name. The type used in this recipe are of the bell variety and are known for their sweet flavor. Vitamins A and C are abundant in peppers, although roasting will deplete some of the vitamin C.

Per Serving: Calories 237; Total Fat 7 g; Saturated Fat 1 g; Cholesterol 2 mg; Sodium 387 mg; Carbohydrate 38 g; Fiber 3 g; Protein 8 g; Calcium 130 mg

Pita Bread Vegetable Pizza

Makes 4 servings

$^1/_2$ cup thinly sliced onion
4 garlic cloves, minced
1 tablespoon olive oil
1 cup sliced mushrooms
$^1/_2$ cup thinly sliced zucchini
$^1/_2$ cup chopped scallions
1 cup chopped red tomato
1 tablespoon chopped fresh basil
1 tablespoon chopped fresh oregano
Salt and pepper to taste
2 pita bread rounds, split horizontally
$^1/_4$ cup shredded Monterey Jack cheese

Method of preparation
▼ Sauté the onion and garlic in the olive oil in a saucepan over medium heat for 5 to 6 minutes. Add the mushrooms, zucchini and scallions and mix well.
▼ Sauté for 5 to 6 minutes. Stir in the tomato.
▼ Simmer for 5 to 6 minutes, stirring occasionally. Remove from heat. Stir in the basil, oregano, salt and pepper.
▼ Preheat the broiler.
▼ Spray both sides of the pita bread with nonstick cooking spray. Arrange on a baking sheet.
▼ Broil until light brown on both sides. Top each pita round with some of the mushroom mixture; sprinkle with the cheese.
▼ Broil just until the cheese melts.

Break your pizza paradigm with this delicious, time-saving selection, substituting Monterey Jack cheese for mozzarella cheese and pita bread for a traditional crust. Pizza is not necessarily junk food, as illustrated in this low-fat, low-sodium version. Almost any vegetable will do as a topper . . . the more, the merrier!

Per Serving: Calories 256; Total Fat 7 g; Saturated Fat 2 g; Cholesterol 6 mg; Sodium 442 mg; Carbohydrate 41 g; Fiber 3 g; Protein 9 g; Calcium 174 mg

Grilled Oysters with Spicy Cajun Sauce

Makes 4 servings

20 oysters in shells, scrubbed
1 slice bacon
1/4 cup minced onion
3/4 teaspoon chili powder
1/4 teaspoon pepper
1/4 teaspoon cumin
1 cup chili sauce
1/2 cup orange juice
3 tablespoons honey
3 tablespoons cider vinegar

Method of preparation

▼ Preheat the grill.
▼ Arrange the oysters on a grill rack 5 to 6 inches above the hot coals and close the grill. Grill for 10 to 12 minutes or until the shells open.
▼ Sauté the bacon in a saucepan over medium heat until brown and crisp. Remove the bacon, reserving the pan drippings. Crumble the bacon.
▼ Sauté the onion in the reserved pan drippings for 5 minutes. Stir in the chili powder, pepper and cumin.
▼ Cook for 5 minutes, stirring frequently. Add the bacon and mix well. Stir in the chili sauce, orange juice, honey and vinegar. Bring to a boil. Remove from heat.
▼ Remove the top shells of the oysters carefully and discard. Arrange the oysters on the half shell on a serving platter. Spoon the cajun sauce over the oysters.

There is one truly outstanding food source of zinc . . . oysters! This mollusk also provides valuable amounts of iron and copper, which along with zinc are often in short supply in many individuals' diets. When purchasing any type of shellfish, be sure to choose those with tightly closed shells or open shells that close when you tap them.

Per Serving: Calories 129; Total Fat 3 g; Saturated Fat 1 g; Cholesterol 38 mg; Sodium 221 mg; Carbohydrate 22 g; Fiber 1 g; Protein 6 g; Calcium 45 mg

Shrimp Cocktail with Gazpacho Sauce

Makes 4 servings

For the shrimp

1 quart water
1 pound (16 to 20 count) shrimp
1 lemon, sliced

For the gazpacho sauce

1 cup chili sauce
1 cup ($1/8$-inch pieces) cucumber
1 cup chopped red tomatoes
$1/4$ cup ($1/8$-inch pieces) green bell
    pepper
$1/4$ cup chopped scallions
$1/2$ cup vegetable stock
1 tablespoon balsamic vinegar
$1/2$ teaspoon curry powder
$1/2$ teaspoon chili powder
1 garlic clove, minced
2 cups shredded romaine

To prepare the shrimp

▼ Bring 1 quart water to a boil in a saucepan over medium heat. Add the shrimp and lemon. Bring to a boil.
▼ Boil for 8 to 10 minutes or until the shrimp turn pink; drain. Chill, covered, in the refrigerator.

To prepare the gazpacho sauce

▼ Combine the chili sauce, cucumber, tomatoes, green pepper, scallions, vegetable stock, balsamic vinegar, curry powder, chili powder and garlic in a bowl and mix well.
▼ Chill, covered, for 45 minutes. May add additional stock for desired consistency.

To assemble

▼ Peel and devein the shrimp.
▼ Place $1/2$ cup lettuce on each of 4 salad plates. Top with the gazpacho sauce.
▼ Arrange 4 or 5 shrimp decoratively around the lettuce. Serve immediately.

An elegant beginning to a meal and a perfect offering if you have a vegetable garden. This gazpacho may also be served as a cold soup if puréed. Use the freshest, ripest vegetables available for extra-brilliant flavors.

Per Serving: Calories 153; Total Fat 2 g; Saturated Fat 0 g; Cholesterol 173 mg; Sodium 185 mg; Carbohydrate 11 g; Fiber 2 g; Protein 25 g; Calcium 100 mg

Spicy Dumplings with Sesame Sauce

Makes 4 servings

For the dough
2 cups flour
3/4 cup water
Salt to taste

For the filling
8 ounces ground turkey
2 tablespoons water
2 tablespoons chopped scallions
1 tablespoons grated gingerroot
1 teaspoon soy sauce

For the sauce
1/3 cup rice vinegar
1/3 cup soy sauce
2 tablespoons tahini
2 tablespoons sugar
1 tablespoon sesame oil
1/2 teaspoon red pepper flakes
2 garlic cloves, minced
2 quarts water

To prepare the dough
▼ Combine the flour, water and salt in a bowl, stirring until the mixture forms a smooth ball. May add additional water as needed.
▼ Chill, covered, for 30 minutes.

To prepare the filling
▼ Combine the turkey, water, scallions, gingerroot and soy sauce in a bowl and mix well.

To prepare the sauce
▼ Combine the rice vinegar, soy sauce, tahini, sugar, sesame oil, red pepper flakes and garlic in a bowl and mix well.

To assemble
▼ Shape the dough into 1-inch balls. Roll each ball into a 4-inch circle on a lightly floured surface.
▼ Spoon 1 teaspoon of the filling in the center of each circle. Moisten the edge of the circle with water; fold to enclose the filling. Pinch the edge to seal. Repeat the process with the remaining dough balls.
▼ Bring 2 quarts water to a boil in a stockpot. Drop the dumplings 1 at a time into the water.
▼ Simmer for 7 to 10 minutes or until the dumplings are firm.
▼ Remove the dumplings with a slotted spoon to a heated platter; drizzle with the sauce. Serve immediately.

Tahini, a light paste consisting of toasted sesame seeds and sesame oil, is used in many Middle Eastern and Oriental dishes. It is similar to peanut butter in consistency. Tahini is quite versatile as a flavoring agent, but is a concentrated source of fat and calories.

Per Serving: Calories 431; Total Fat 13 g; Saturated Fat 2 g; Cholesterol 45 mg; Sodium 1232 mg; Carbohydrate 60 g; Fiber 1 g; Protein 19 g; Calcium 104 mg

Thai-Style Turkey Lettuce Rolls

Makes 4 servings

For the turkey rolls

1 ounce mung bean threads
8 ounces ground turkey
1 teaspoon sesame oil
1 cup minced celery
$1/2$ cup bean sprouts
$1/2$ cup sliced shiitake mushrooms
$1^1/2$ tablespoons soy sauce
1 tablespoon chopped fresh basil
2 heads Boston lettuce, separated into
   leaves

For the dipping sauce

3 tablespoons soy sauce
2 tablespoons rice vinegar
1 teaspoon hoisin sauce
1 teaspoon sesame oil
1 garlic clove, minced

To prepare the turkey rolls

▼ Soak the bean threads with enough hot water to cover in a bowl until softened; drain.
▼ Sauté the turkey in the sesame oil in a nonstick skillet over medium heat for 5 minutes.
   Add the celery, bean sprouts and mushrooms.
▼ Sauté for 3 to 4 minutes. Remove from heat. Let stand until cool.
▼ Combine the turkey mixture, bean threads, soy sauce and basil in a bowl and
   mix well.

To prepare the dipping sauce

▼ Combine the soy sauce, rice vinegar, hoisin sauce, sesame oil and garlic in a bowl
   and mix well.

To assemble

▼ Place a lettuce leaf on a flat surface. Spoon 2 tablespoons of the turkey mixture on
   one end of the lettuce leaf. Fold in the sides and roll tightly to enclose the filling.
   Place in a dish. Repeat the process with the remaining filling and lettuce leaves; will
   yield 8 rolls.
▼ Chill the rolls for 10 minutes. Cut each roll diagonally into halves. Arrange on a chilled
   platter. Serve with the dipping sauce.

Traditionally made with ground pork, this recipe substitutes turkey to reduce
the fat content by 7 grams. When purchasing ground turkey, be aware that it
may not be as lean as one might expect. The skin and fat are often ground
along with the meat. Ask your butcher to grind skinless turkey breast in order to further
decrease the fat content.

Per Serving: Calories 213; Total Fat 8 g; Saturated Fat 2 g; Cholesterol 45 mg; Sodium 1028 mg;
Carbohydrate 24 g; Fiber 5 g; Protein 16 g; Calcium 114 mg

Shredded Spicy Beef Soup

Makes 4 servings

2 ounces mung bean threads
8 ounces lean beef, shredded
1 teaspoon chili paste
1 teaspoon sesame oil
$1/2$ teaspoon five-spice powder
5 cups chicken stock
1 cup sliced shiitake mushrooms
$1/2$ cup julienned snow peas
$1/2$ cup julienned carrot
$1/4$ cup chopped scallions
$1/4$ cup sherry
1 stalk lemon grass, chopped

Method of preparation
▼ Soak the bean threads in enough hot water to cover in a bowl until softened; drain.
▼ Combine the beef, chili paste, sesame oil and five-spice powder in a bowl and mix well. Let stand for 20 minutes.
▼ Sauté the beef mixture in a skillet over medium heat until brown. Add the stock, mushrooms, snow peas, carrot, scallions, sherry and lemon grass and mix well. Bring to a simmer.
▼ Simmer for 5 to 10 minutes or until of the desired consistency, stirring frequently. Stir in the bean threads.
▼ Ladle into heated soup bowls. Serve immediately.

A desirable flavoring in soups and salads, lemon grass can be found in most gourmet stores or supermarkets. Native to Southeast Asia where lemons are not always available, the citric oils in the lemon grass convey the flavor of lemon. If lemon grass is not available, add a small amount of lemon zest.

Per Serving: Calories 233; Total Fat 5 g; Saturated Fat 1 g; Cholesterol 33 mg; Sodium 129 mg; Carbohydrate 30 g; Fiber 4 g; Protein 16 g; Calcium 24 mg

Old-Fashioned Black Bean Soup

Makes 4 servings

For the soup

1/2 cup dried black beans
1 quart water
5 cups chicken stock
1/2 cup chopped red onion
1/2 cup chopped carrot
2 teaspoons cumin
2 teaspoons chili powder
3 garlic cloves, minced
1/2 cup chopped extra-lean ham

For the topping

1 cup chopped red tomato
1/4 cup chopped red onion
1/4 cup chopped green bell pepper
Salt and pepper to taste

To prepare the soup

▼ Sort and rinse the black beans. Combine the beans, water, stock, red onion, carrot, cumin, chili powder and garlic in a stockpot. Bring to a boil; reduce heat.
▼ Simmer for 1 1/2 to 2 hours or until the beans are tender, stirring occasionally. Stir in the ham.
▼ Simmer for 20 minutes, stirring occasionally.
▼ Process the mixture in a food processor until puréed. Press the purée with a rubber spatula through a strainer into a bowl. May add additional chicken stock for the desired consistency. Return the soup to the stockpot.
▼ Cook just until heated through, stirring constantly.

To prepare the topping

▼ Combine the tomato, red onion, green pepper, salt and pepper in a bowl and mix well.

To assemble

▼ Ladle the soup into heated bowls. Sprinkle with the topping.
▼ Serve immediately.

The best-tasting soups are made with fresh stock, so we have included recipes for chicken stock on page 164 and vegetable stock on page 165 for your use. Soups are a great way of sneaking vegetables into loved ones without them noticing. In addition to the protein provided by the beans and ham, each diner will get a little more than one of the recommended five daily servings of fruits and vegetables.

Per Serving: Calories 169; Total Fat 3 g; Saturated Fat 1 g; Cholesterol 14 mg; Sodium 448 mg; Carbohydrate 24 g; Fiber 6 g; Protein 13 g; Calcium 63 mg

Hearty Cabbage Soup with Dill Spaetzle

Makes 4 servings

For the soup

5 cups chicken stock
$1^1/_2$ cups shredded savoy cabbage
$^1/_2$ cup sliced onion
$^1/_2$ cup chopped red tomato
$^1/_2$ cup chopped celery
$^1/_2$ teaspoon caraway seeds
Salt and pepper to taste

For the spaetzle

2 cups water
2 cups flour
$^1/_2$ cup skim milk
$^1/_2$ cup water
2 eggs, beaten
2 tablespoons chopped fresh dillweed
$^1/_2$ teaspoon salt

To prepare the soup

▼ Bring the stock to a boil in a stockpot. Add the cabbage, onion, tomato, celery and caraway seeds. Bring to a boil. Add salt and pepper and mix well. Set aside.

To prepare the spaetzle

▼ Bring 2 cups water to a boil in a stockpot.
▼ Combine the flour, skim milk, $^1/_2$ cup water, eggs, dillweed and salt in a bowl, stirring until of the consistency of a thick batter.
▼ Place a colander over but not touching the boiling water. Pour the batter into the colander; force through with a rubber spatula.
▼ Cook until the spaetzle float to the surface. Remove the spaetzle with a slotted spoon to the soup.
▼ Bring the soup to a boil. Ladle into heated soup bowls. Serve immediately.

Hearty and oh so healthy! Members of the cabbage family, including broccoli, cauliflower, brussels sprouts, and kale, contain indoles that may help prevent the development of cancer. These substances act as cancer-blocking agents, preventing cancer-causing chemicals from damaging cells.

Per Serving: Calories 306; Total Fat 4 g; Saturated Fat 1 g; Cholesterol 107 mg; Sodium 416 mg; Carbohydrate 55 g; Fiber 2 g; Protein 13 g; Calcium 118 mg

Chicken Soup Southwestern-Style

Makes 4 servings

12 ounces boneless skinless chicken breasts
1 tablespoon olive oil
1 cup chopped red onion
1/2 cup chopped red bell pepper
1/4 cup chopped carrot
2 poblano peppers, chopped
4 garlic cloves, minced
1 cup chopped red tomato
4 tomatillos, chopped
5 cups chicken stock
Salt and pepper to taste

Method of preparation
▼ Rinse the chicken and pat dry. Cut into 1/4-inch pieces.
▼ Heat the olive oil in a stockpot over medium heat. Add the chicken.
▼ Sauté for 2 to 3 minutes. Stir in the red onion, red pepper, carrot, poblano peppers and garlic.
▼ Sauté for 5 minutes. Stir in the tomato and tomatillos.
▼ Sauté for 1 minute. Add the stock and mix well. Bring to a boil; reduce heat.
▼ Simmer for 25 minutes, stirring occasionally. Season with salt and pepper.
▼ Ladle into heated soup bowls. Serve immediately.

Tomatillos, small hard green fruits that are covered with a paper-like husk, require peeling before cooking. Resembling fat green cherry tomatoes, their flavor is a bit tart. If fresh varieties are not available, canned selections are often obtainable.

Per Serving: Calories 193; Total Fat 6 g; Saturated Fat 1 g; Cholesterol 49 mg; Sodium 69 mg; Carbohydrate 13 g; Fiber 3 g; Protein 23 g; Calcium 39 mg

Roasted Garlic Soup
with Shiitake Mushrooms

Makes 4 servings

12 unpeeled garlic cloves
1 tablespoon olive oil
5 cups chicken stock
2 cups chopped peeled potatoes
$1/2$ cup brandy
1 cup sliced shiitake mushrooms
1 teaspoon thyme
$1/2$ teaspoon rosemary
$1/2$ cup plain nonfat yogurt
2 tablespoons chopped fresh parsley

Method of preparation
▼ Preheat the oven to 400 degrees.
▼ Combine the garlic and olive oil in a roasting pan and mix well. Roast for 15 minutes or until tender. Let stand until cool.
▼ Bring the stock, potatoes and brandy to a boil in a stockpot; reduce the heat.
▼ Simmer for 30 to 35 minutes or until the potatoes are tender, stirring occasionally. Squeeze the garlic into the stock mixture, discarding the skins.
▼ Simmer for 10 minutes, stirring occasionally. Strain into a saucepan. Press the garlic and potatoes with a rubber spatula through the strainer into a saucepan. Stir in the mushrooms, thyme and rosemary.
▼ Simmer for 10 minutes, stirring occasionally. Remove from heat. Stir in the yogurt and parsley.
▼ Ladle into heated soup bowls. Serve immediately.

Twelve garlic cloves! Yes, when roasted, the flavor of garlic becomes mild and sweet tasting. It has been suggested that garlic may provide health benefits, ranging from protection against heart disease to antibiotic properties. Food lovers rejoice, since the health benefits of garlic are based on the use of fresh garlic and not pills.

Per Serving: Calories 225; Total Fat 4 g; Saturated Fat 1 g; Cholesterol 0 mg; Sodium 37 mg; Carbohydrate 27 g; Fiber 3 g; Protein 6 g; Calcium 116 mg

Country Minestrone

Makes 4 servings

1 tablespoon olive oil
1 cup sliced leeks
2 garlic cloves, minced
4 cups chicken stock
1 cup chopped peeled potatoes
$1/2$ cup chopped red tomato
2 cups chopped savoy cabbage
1 cup chopped zucchini
1 tablespoon minced fresh rosemary
1 teaspoon minced fresh thyme
1 (16-ounce) can white beans, drained, rinsed
1 tablespoon grated Parmesan cheese
Salt and pepper to taste

Method of preparation
▼ Heat the olive oil in a stockpot over medium heat until hot. Add the leeks and garlic and mix well.
▼ Sauté for 3 to 4 minutes or until the leeks wilt. Add the stock, potatoes and tomato and mix well. Bring to a boil; reduce heat.
▼ Simmer for 25 minutes or just until the potatoes are tender, stirring occasionally. Stir in the cabbage, zucchini, rosemary and thyme. Bring to a boil; reduce heat.
▼ Simmer for 10 minutes, stirring occasionally. Add the white beans, cheese, salt and pepper and mix well.
▼ Ladle into heated soup bowls. Serve immediately.

Minestrone is an Italian soup made with a variety of vegetables. Don't be afraid to veer from the recipe and add whatever vegetables are in season. For a change, ladle over dry bread heated until crispy.

Per Serving: Calories 270; Total Fat 5 g; Saturated Fat 1 g; Cholesterol 1 mg; Sodium 50 mg;
Carbohydrate 44 g; Fiber 10 g; Protein 15 g; Calcium 190 mg

Creamy Seafood Corn Chowder

Makes 4 servings

1 tablespoon butter
1 cup chopped red bell peppers
$1/2$ cup chopped scallions
3 tablespoons flour
4 cups skim milk
1 cup clam broth
1 cup chopped potatoes
4 ounces shrimp, peeled, deveined
4 ounces bay scallops, sliced
1 cup whole kernel corn
3 tablespoons sherry
1 teaspoon chopped fresh thyme
Salt and pepper to taste

Method of preparation

▼ Heat the butter in a stockpot over medium heat until melted. Add the red peppers and scallions and mix well.
▼ Sauté for 3 to 4 minutes. Stir in the flour. Add the skim milk and clam broth gradually, whisking until mixed. Stir in the potatoes, shrimp and scallops.
▼ Simmer for 25 minutes or until the potatoes are tender, stirring occasionally. Add the corn, sherry, thyme, salt and pepper and mix well.
▼ Ladle into heated soup bowls. Serve immediately.

A very simple yet elegant creation, this chowder could certainly be served as the main course for a luncheon. A creative way to incorporate one of the two daily recommended servings of milk into your diet.

Per Serving: Calories 274; Total Fat 5 g; Saturated Fat 2 g; Cholesterol 65 mg; Sodium 249 mg; Carbohydrate 34 g; Fiber 2 g; Protein 23 g; Calcium 348 mg

Purée of Butternut Squash and Apple Soup

Makes 4 servings

5 cups chicken stock
5 cups chopped peeled butternut squash
1 tablespoon minced onion
1 tablespoon minced celery
1 cup plain nonfat yogurt
1 cup shredded peeled Granny Smith apple
1 teaspoon sugar
1/4 teaspoon nutmeg
1/4 teaspoon cinnamon

Method of preparation

▼ Bring the stock to a boil in a stockpot. Add the squash, onion and celery.
▼ Simmer for 30 to 40 minutes or until the squash is tender. Drain, reserving the broth.
▼ Process the squash in a food processor until puréed. Add to the reserved broth. Bring to a boil. Remove from heat. Stir in the yogurt, apple, sugar, nutmeg and cinnamon.
▼ Ladle into heated soup bowls. Serve immediately.

How can anyone not like butternut squash? Significantly rich in vitamin A, delectable in flavor, and easily stored for months in a cool place, butternut tops the list of winter squash varieties. Avoid purchasing squash that have watery spots, which indicate decay.

Per Serving: Calories 137; Total Fat 1 g; Saturated Fat 0 g; Cholesterol 1 mg; Sodium 62 mg; Carbohydrate 30 g; Fiber 1 g; Protein 6 g; Calcium 204 mg

Spicy Vegetable Cheese Chili

Makes 4 servings

1 tablespoon olive oil
1/2 cup chopped celery
1/2 cup chopped green bell pepper
1/2 cup chopped onion
2 garlic cloves, minced
1 1/2 cups chopped tomatoes
1 (12-ounce) can beer
1 cup cooked kidney beans
2 tablespoons wine vinegar
1 tablespoon chopped jalapeño
1 tablespoon chili powder
1 teaspoon cumin
1 teaspoon oregano
1/2 teaspoon allspice
1/2 teaspoon cayenne
1/2 cup shredded low-fat Vermont Cheddar cheese

Method of preparation

▼ Heat the olive oil in a heavy saucepan. Add the celery, green pepper, onion and garlic.
▼ Sauté for 5 minutes. Add the tomatoes and mix well.
▼ Simmer for 10 minutes, stirring occasionally. Stir in the beer, kidney beans, wine vinegar, jalapeño, chili powder, cumin, oregano, allspice and cayenne.
▼ Simmer for 15 to 20 minutes or until of the desired consistency, stirring occasionally.
▼ Ladle into heated chili bowls. Sprinkle with the cheese. Serve immediately.

Beans are essential in any chili recipe. Kidney beans are generally used, although black beans or pinto beans are acceptable. If you're not a regular "bean eater," introduce them gradually into your diet in order to avoid excessive flatulence or gas. The flavor of this dish is enhanced if prepared one day in advance and reheated just before serving.

Per Serving: Calories 199; Total Fat 5 g; Saturated Fat 1 g; Cholesterol 3 mg; Sodium 207 mg; Carbohydrate 22 g; Fiber 5 g; Protein 9 g; Calcium 157 mg

Vichyssoise of Carrot and Ginger

Makes 4 servings

1 tablespoon butter
2 cups chopped peeled carrots
$^1/_2$ cup chopped leek
$1^1/_2$ cups chopped peeled potatoes
1 garlic clove, chopped
1 teaspoon grated gingerroot
4 cups chicken stock
$^1/_2$ cup plain nonfat yogurt
Salt and pepper to taste

Method of preparation

▼ Heat the butter in a stockpot over medium heat until melted. Add the carrots and leek.
▼ Sauté for 10 minutes, stirring constantly. Add the potatoes, garlic and gingerroot and mix well.
▼ Sauté for 1 minute. Stir in the stock.
▼ Simmer for 30 minutes or until the carrots and potatoes are tender, stirring occasionally. Drain, reserving the stock.
▼ Purée the vegetables in a food processor fitted with a steel blade. Return the puréed vegetables to the reserved stock. Bring to a boil. Remove from heat. Stir in the yogurt, salt and pepper.
▼ Ladle into heated soup bowls. Serve immediately.

Vichyssoise (pronounce the last "s" like a "z") is a velvety smooth soup that can be served either hot or cold. Generally made with potatoes or leeks, this version utilizes both, plus the economical beta-carotene-rich carrot. Pungent ginger is most flavorful when used fresh, although a smaller amount of dried ginger may be used.

Per Serving: Calories 112; Total Fat 3 g; Saturated Fat 2 g; Cholesterol 8 mg; Sodium 78 mg; Carbohydrate 17 g; Fiber 3 g; Protein 4 g; Calcium 92 mg

Santa Fe Chicken Salad

Makes 4 servings

For the chicken

1 pound boneless skinless chicken breast
  halves
2 tablespoons lime juice
2 tablespoons minced jalapeño
1 tablespoon olive oil
1 tablespoon honey
1 tablespoon prepared mustard
1 teaspoon chili powder
1 teaspoon cumin

For the salad

6 cups chopped romaine
1 cup chopped red tomato
1 cup chopped scallions
2 tablespoons red wine vinegar
1 1/2 tablespoons olive oil
1/2 teaspoon chili powder
1/4 teaspoon cumin
Salt and pepper to taste

To prepare the chicken

▼ Rinse the chicken and pat dry. Arrange in a glass dish.
▼ Pour a mixture of the lime juice, jalapeño, olive oil, honey, mustard, chili powder and cumin over the chicken, turning to coat.
▼ Marinate in the refrigerator for 1 hour, turning occasionally.
▼ Spray a cold grill rack with nonstick cooking spray and place the rack 5 to 6 inches above coals. Preheat the grill.
▼ Drain the chicken, reserving the marinade. Grill the chicken 7 to 8 minutes per side or until cooked through, basting frequently with the reserved marinade. Slice the chicken into julienned strips.

To prepare the salad

▼ Combine the romaine, tomato and scallions in a bowl and mix gently. Add a mixture of the wine vinegar, olive oil, chili powder, cumin, salt and pepper, tossing to coat.

To assemble

▼ Spoon the salad onto a chilled serving platter. Arrange the chicken decoratively around the salad. Serve immediately.

Very common ingredients can make for an uncommonly good meal. The honey mustard based marinade goes Southwest with the addition of chili powder and cumin. Perfect for a luncheon salad or a light summer meal.

Per Serving: Calories 264; Total Fat 11 g; Saturated Fat 2 g; Cholesterol 66 mg; Sodium 150 mg;
Carbohydrate 13 g; Fiber 4 g; Protein 29 g; Calcium 78 mg
Nutritional profile includes entire amount of marinade.

Thai Noodle Salad

Makes 4 servings

For the dressing

2 tablespoons sugar
2 tablespoons soy sauce
1 tablespoon sesame oil
1 teaspoon grated gingerroot
1/2 teaspoon hot pepper sauce

For the chicken

1 pound boneless skinless chicken breasts
2 tablespoons brown sugar
2 tablespoons soy sauce
2 tablespoons sake
1 tablespoon hoisin sauce

For the salad

2 ounces mung bean threads
1 cup julienned carrot
1 cup julienned pea pods
1/2 cup chopped scallions

To prepare the dressing

▼ Combine the sugar, soy sauce, sesame oil, gingerroot and hot pepper sauce in a small jar with a tightfitting lid, shaking to mix. Chill in the refrigerator.

To prepare the salad

▼ Soak the mung bean threads in enough hot water to cover in a bowl until softened; drain.
▼ Combine the bean threads, carrot, pea pods and scallions in a bowl and mix gently. Chill, covered, in the refrigerator.

To prepare the chicken

▼ Rinse the chicken and pat dry. Slice into 1/2-inch strips. Combine the chicken with a mixture of the brown sugar, soy sauce, sake and hoisin sauce in a bowl and mix well.
▼ Marinate in the refrigerator for 30 minutes, turning occasionally. Drain, discarding the marinade.
▼ Sauté the chicken in a nonstick pan over medium heat for 10 to 12 minutes or until the chicken is cooked through, stirring constantly.

To assemble

▼ Arrange the salad on a serving platter. Top with the chicken; drizzle with the dressing.
▼ Serve immediately.

Only available in Oriental markets in the past, pea pods are now easily found in the fresh and frozen sections of large supermarkets. Preparation of pea pods, which are rich in vitamin C and folate, includes cutting off the ends and removing any strings.

Per Serving: Calories 308; Total Fat 6 g; Saturated Fat 1 g; Cholesterol 66 mg; Sodium 921 mg;
Carbohydrate 33 g; Fiber 3 g; Protein 29 g; Calcium 53 mg
Nutritional profile includes the entire amount of marinade.

Pan-Seared Shrimp Salad with Roasted Garlic Dressing

Makes 4 servings

For the dressing

6 unpeeled garlic cloves
2 1/2 tablespoons olive oil
2 tablespoons white wine vinegar
2 tablespoons lime juice
1 tablespoon minced onion
1 tablespoon honey

For the salad

4 cups mesclun greens
1 pound shrimp, peeled, deveined
1/2 teaspoon chili powder
1/4 teaspoon cumin
1/8 teaspoon coriander
Salt and pepper to taste

To prepare the dressing

▼ Preheat the oven to 400 degrees.
▼ Combine the garlic and 1 tablespoon of the olive oil in a baking pan and mix well.
▼ Roast for 10 to 15 minutes or until the garlic is tender. Squeeze the garlic into a saucepan, discarding the skins. Add the remaining olive oil, wine vinegar, lime juice, onion and honey and mix well.

To prepare the salad

▼ Arrange the greens on 4 salad plates. Chill in the refrigerator.
▼ Combine the shrimp, chili powder, cumin, coriander, salt and pepper in a bowl, turning to coat.
▼ Marinate in the refrigerator for 30 minutes, turning occasionally.
▼ Heat a sauté pan sprayed with nonstick cooking spray until hot. Add the shrimp.
▼ Sauté for 3 to 4 minutes per side or until the shrimp turn pink. Remove the shrimp to a platter.
▼ Add the dressing to the sauté pan. Whisk until heated through; do not boil.

To assemble

▼ Arrange the shrimp over the chilled greens; drizzle with the warm dressing.

Cumin and coriander are often found in the same recipe since their flavors tend to complement each other. Cumin is grown in near-tropical conditions, while coriander plants grow in more temperate climates. Both are available in the dried form.

Per Serving: Calories 232; Total Fat 11 g; Saturated Fat 2 g; Cholesterol 173 mg; Sodium 186 mg; Carbohydrate 10 g; Fiber 2 g; Protein 24 g; Calcium 92 mg

Pan-Seared Sesame and Peppercorn-Crusted Tuna Salad

Makes 4 servings

For the dressing
2 tablespoons olive oil
2 tablespoons lemon juice
1 tablespoon chopped fresh basil
1 teaspoon Dijon mustard
1/4 teaspoon sugar
Salt and pepper to taste

For the salad
2 cups torn romaine
1 cup chopped frisee
1 cup chopped radicchio
1 cup julienned Belgian endive
2 (8-ounce) tuna steaks
1 tablespoon crushed peppercorns
1 tablespoon sesame seeds

To prepare the dressing
▼ Combine the olive oil, lemon juice, basil, Dijon mustard, sugar, salt and pepper in a jar with a tightfitting lid, shaking to mix.

To prepare the salad
▼ Toss the romaine, frisee, radicchio and Belgian endive in a bowl. Arrange on a chilled platter.
▼ Heat a nonstick skillet over medium heat. Spray both sides of the tuna steaks lightly with nonstick cooking spray. Sprinkle both sides with the peppercorns and sesame seeds; press lightly.
▼ Sear the steaks in the prepared skillet for 3 to 4 minutes per side or until done to taste.

To assemble
▼ Cut the tuna into 1/4-inch slices.
▼ Arrange the tuna around the salad greens; drizzle with the dressing. Serve immediately.

There is more to lettuce than iceberg alone. Numerous varieties of leafy greens are now available in most supermarkets. Romaine, frisee, red leaf, buttercrunch, and Bibb are but a few of the tastier and more nutritious varieties. A good rule of thumb . . . the darker the leaves, whether green or red, the more nutritious. All varieties are a good source of fiber.

Per Serving: Calories 263; Total Fat 14 g; Saturated Fat 3 g; Cholesterol 43 mg; Sodium 82 mg; Carbohydrate 5 g; Fiber 3 g; Protein 29 g; Calcium 73 mg

Tuscan Bean and Bread Salad

Makes 4 servings

For the dressing

1 cup cooked peas
1/2 cup chopped red tomato
1/2 cup chopped red onion
2 tablespoons olive oil
2 tablespoons minced fresh parsley
2 tablespoons lemon juice
3 garlic cloves, minced
Salt and pepper to taste

For the salad

12 ounces dried navy beans
6 cups water
3 bay leaves
1 teaspoon oregano
4 slices sourdough bread, toasted

To prepare the dressing
▼ Combine the peas, tomato, red onion, olive oil, parsley, lemon juice, garlic, salt and pepper in a bowl and mix gently.

To prepare the salad
▼ Sort and rinse the navy beans. Combine the navy beans, water, bay leaves and oregano in a stockpot. Bring to a boil; reduce heat.
▼ Simmer for 1 1/2 hours or until the beans are tender, stirring occasionally. Drain, discarding the bay leaves and liquid.
▼ Add the hot beans to the dressing and mix well. Chill for 30 minutes.

To assemble
▼ Place 1 slice of sourdough bread on each of 4 salad plates. Spoon the bean mixture over the bread.
▼ Serve immediately.

This is a filling salad that can easily be served as a luncheon or dinner entrée. If the salad is eaten for dinner, the feeling of fullness that follows feasting on beans may help to curb those late-night snack yearnings. Also, research shows that eating beans may help to control diabetes.

Per Serving: Calories 483; Total Fat 9 g; Saturated Fat 1 g; Cholesterol 0 mg; Sodium 190 mg; Carbohydrate 79 g; Fiber 25 g; Protein 25 g; Calcium 215 mg

Couscous Salad with Pink Lentils

Makes 4 servings

$1/2$ cup pink lentils
$12/3$ cups chicken stock
1 cup couscous
$1/2$ cup shredded zucchini
$1/2$ cup shredded carrot
$1/4$ cup chopped green bell pepper
$1/4$ cup chopped red bell pepper
$1/4$ cup chopped red onion
2 tablespoons raisins
3 tablespoons lemon juice
2 tablespoons olive oil
$1/2$ teaspoon pepper
1 teaspoon minced fresh basil
1 teaspoon minced fresh thyme
$1/2$ teaspoon salt
2 cups shredded romaine

Method of preparation

▼ Sort and rinse the lentils. Combine the lentils with enough water to cover in a saucepan. Bring to a boil; reduce heat.
▼ Simmer for 30 minutes, stirring occasionally; drain. Let stand until cool.
▼ Bring the stock to a boil in a saucepan. Stir in the couscous. Remove from heat. Let stand, covered, for 10 minutes.
▼ Combine the zucchini, carrot, green pepper, red pepper, red onion and raisins in a bowl and mix gently. Stir in a mixture of the lemon juice, olive oil, pepper, basil, thyme and salt. Add the lentils and couscous and mix well.
▼ Chill, covered, in the refrigerator.
▼ Arrange the romaine on a chilled serving platter. Spoon the couscous mixture over the romaine. Serve immediately.

Couscous (pronounced koose-koose) is made from finely ground semolina and is a staple in North Africa. An alternative to noodles and rice, couscous is a rich source of carbohydrates. Most notable about this grain is its quick-cooking time. Actually, it is not cooked at all. Just boil the liquid, stir in the couscous, cover, and remove from the heat. That's fast food!

Per Serving: Calories 355; Total Fat 8 g; Saturated Fat 1 g; Cholesterol 0 mg; Sodium 283 mg; Carbohydrate 59 g; Fiber 12 g; Protein 14 g; Calcium 52 mg

Greek Pasta Salad

Makes 4 servings

For the dressing

1 1/2 cups plain nonfat yogurt
3/4 cup crumbled feta cheese
2 garlic cloves, minced
2 tablespoons minced fresh cilantro
2 tablespoons minced fresh basil
2 tablespoons minced fresh parsley
2 tablespoons lemon juice
2 teaspoons minced jalapeño
Salt and pepper to taste

For the salad

1 (8-ounce) package rotini, cooked, drained
1 cup chopped cucumber
1 cup chopped red tomato
1 cup chopped red onion
1/2 cup chopped scallions

To prepare the dressing

▼ Combine the yogurt, feta cheese, garlic, cilantro, basil, parsley, lemon juice, jalapeño, salt and pepper in a bowl and mix gently.

To prepare the salad

▼ Combine the rotini, cucumber, tomato, red onion and scallions in a bowl and mix well.

To assemble

▼ Combine the rotini mixture and dressing in a bowl, tossing to coat.
▼ Spoon onto a chilled serving platter. Serve immediately.

Feta cheese is made from sheep or goat milk, and is slightly lower in fat than some cheeses made from cow's milk. It is cured and stored in brine, and consequently is quite salty. To reduce the salt content, soak the cheese in water. Discard the water and the result is a feta cheese lower in sodium.

Per Serving: Calories 353; Total Fat 6 g; Saturated Fat 4 g; Cholesterol 20 mg; Sodium 318 mg; Carbohydrate 59 g; Fiber 3 g; Protein 17 g; Calcium 325 mg

Roasted Red Bliss Potato Salad

Makes 4 servings

2 pounds unpeeled red potatoes, sliced
$1/2$ teaspoon salt
1 tablespoon olive oil
$1/2$ cup chopped red bell pepper
$1^1/_2$ tablespoons minced shallot
1 teaspoon minced fresh tarragon
1 teaspoon paprika
$1/2$ teaspoon minced fresh rosemary
2 tablespoons lemon juice
1 tablespoon chopped fresh parsley
2 garlic cloves, minced

Method of preparation
▼ Preheat the oven to 400 degrees.
▼ Sauté the potatoes and salt in the olive oil in a nonstick skillet over medium heat for 5 to 6 minutes. Remove from heat. Stir in the red pepper, shallot, tarragon, paprika and rosemary. Spoon into a baking dish.
▼ Bake for 30 minutes or until the potatoes are tender. Spoon onto a heated platter. Drizzle with the lemon juice; sprinkle with the parsley and garlic.
▼ Serve at room temperature.

Potatoes are not fattening! A medium-size potato has approximately 100 calories, virtually no fat, and is chock-full of potassium and vitamin C. By retaining the skin you reap the benefits of its fiber content and add to the dish's attractiveness. Be wary of what you put on top of potatoes, but the potato itself is very nutritious.

Per Serving: Calories 222; Total Fat 4 g; Saturated Fat 1 g; Cholesterol 0 mg; Sodium 282 mg; Carbohydrate 44 g; Fiber 4 g; Protein 5 g; Calcium 25 mg

Un-Classic Spinach Salad

Makes 4 servings

For the salad

6 cups spinach leaves, stems removed
1 cup sliced fresh mushrooms
1 cup julienned red bell pepper
1 cup julienned yellow squash
1 cup chopped tofu
1/2 cup julienned red onion
2 tablespoons grated Parmesan cheese

For the dressing

3 tablespoons balsamic vinegar
2 tablespoons olive oil
2 tablespoons ketchup
1/2 teaspoon brown sugar
1 garlic clove, minced
Salt and pepper to taste

To prepare the salad

▼ Combine the spinach, mushrooms, red pepper, squash, tofu, red onion and cheese in a serving bowl and toss gently.
▼ Chill, covered, in the refrigerator.

To prepare the dressing

▼ Combine the balsamic vinegar, olive oil, ketchup, brown sugar, garlic, salt and pepper in a blender container.
▼ Process on high until blended.

To assemble

▼ Drizzle the dressing over the chilled salad, tossing to coat.
▼ Serve immediately.

This spinach medley is a colorful, tasty, fiber- and vitamin-rich alternative to lettuce-based salads and is substantial enough to serve for luncheons. Its nutritional detraction is oxalic acid, which can bind minerals such as calcium and iron, making them unavailable for absorption by the body. Not to worry . . . a well-balanced diet usually compensates.

Per Serving: Calories 164; Total Fat 10 g; Saturated Fat 2 g; Cholesterol 2 mg; Sodium 208 mg; Carbohydrate 13 g; Fiber 5 g; Protein 9 g; Calcium 187 mg

Grilled Mediterranean Salad with Plum Tomato Vinaigrette

Makes 4 servings

For the dressing

1/2 cup chopped seeded plum tomatoes
3 tablespoons lemon juice
1 tablespoon lime juice
1 tablespoon chopped fresh oregano
2 teaspoons olive oil
Salt and pepper to taste

For the salad

1 eggplant, cut into 1/4-inch slices
2 zucchini, cut into 1/4-inch slices
1 yellow squash, cut into 1/4-inch slices
1 cup (1/4-inch slices) red bell pepper
1 cup (1/4-inch slices) green bell pepper
1 cup (1/4-inch slices) red onion
4 red tomatoes, cut into 1/4-inch slices
3/4 cup crumbled feta cheese
1 head romaine, trimmed

For the dressing

▼ Process the plum tomatoes, lemon juice, lime juice, oregano, olive oil, salt and pepper in a food processor until puréed.

For the salad

▼ Spray a cold grill rack with nonstick cooking spray. Preheat the grill.
▼ Grill the eggplant, zucchini and yellow squash for 1 minute per side. Remove to a platter.
▼ Grill the red and green peppers for 2 to 3 minutes or until tender, turning occasionally. Remove to the platter.
▼ Grill the onion for 2 to 3 minutes; do not separate the slices. Remove to the platter.
▼ Grill the tomatoes for 1 minute or until done to taste; do not overcook. Remove to the platter.

To assemble

▼ Line a loaf pan with plastic wrap, allowing the plastic wrap to hang over the side. Reserve a small amount of dressing for the topping. Layer the eggplant, zucchini, yellow squash, dressing, feta cheese, bell peppers, red onion, tomatoes, dressing and feta cheese alternately in the prepared pan until all the ingredients are used; drizzle with the reserved dressing.
▼ Fold the plastic wrap over to cover the pan; press firmly to compact the vegetables. Chill for 1 hour.
▼ Invert onto a chilled serving platter. Surround with the romaine.

Containing eleven grams of fiber, this salad provides half the National Cancer Institute's twenty- to thirty-gram daily recommendation. Fiber, plant material that cannot be digested by humans, is calorie-free. Of interest to waistline watchers, fiber creates a feeling of fullness, helping to enhance satiety.

Per Serving: Calories 209; Total Fat 8 g; Saturated Fat 4 g; Cholesterol 19 mg; Sodium 270 mg; Carbohydrate 30 g; Fiber 11 g; Protein 10 g; Calcium 216 mg

Since most people do plan their entrée around a meat item, we must ask the question . . . Why is the subject of meat in a healthful diet usually discussed as an all-or-nothing proposition? You *can* have meat, if you choose to, and still adhere to current health guidelines.

The paradigm you may need to rethink is **how much** meat you are using in your entrées. There was a time, not too long ago, when it was common to plan meals around an eight- to twelve-ounce meat portion. If you're willing to break that paradigm and use less meat, the wonderful tastes of beef, pork, and lamb can still be a part of your healthful dining experience. Explore our selections of Crispy Beef with Portobellos, Spezzatino di Maiale, and Lamb Vindaloo with Lentils.

All of the entrées in this section have approximately six-ounce portions of meat, sometimes a little less, sometimes a little more. At first, this may sound like a miniature portion, but have faith. These recipes are satisfying, especially when combined with a selection from the appetizers, soups, salads, accompaniments, and desserts.

The main nutritional focus when evaluating meat-centered entrées is generally the amount of fat they contain. Some of the following entrées may be a little higher in fat than you usually prefer. Remember that you should evaluate your food intake over the course of a whole day or series of days and not solely on one entrée or meal. If you choose to prepare an entrée on the higher-fat side, focus on accompaniments that are on the low-fat side. Also, plan the rest of your day's meals on a low-fat slant.

Although entrées are traditionally meat centered, additional entrée selections including poultry, seafood, and pasta are presented. Also worth considering is breaking the pattern of the traditional entrée-oriented paradigm by offering a soup and a salad as the focal point of a meal.

REPAST

™

MEATS

POULTRY

SEAFOOD

PASTA

Grilled Flank Steak with Red Wine Sauce

Wine: Bordeaux   Makes 4 servings

2 cups low-sodium beef broth
2 cups red wine
$1/2$ cup minced shallots
Salt and pepper to taste
2 tablespoons garlic paste, roasted
$1/4$ cup chopped fresh parsley
1 (16-ounce) flank steak, trimmed

Method of preparation
▼ Preheat the grill until hot.
▼ Combine the beef broth, wine, shallots, salt, pepper, half the garlic paste and half the parsley in a large saucepan. Cook until reduced by $1/2$. Process in a food processor until smooth.
▼ Mix the remaining garlic paste and parsley in a small bowl. Stir in 2 tablespoons of the wine sauce, reserving the remaining wine sauce for another steak.
▼ Place the steak on the grill 4 inches above the hot coals. Grill for 5 to 6 minutes for medium-rare.
▼ Brush the steak with the wine sauce. Place on a cutting board and slice diagonally into $1/8$-inch thick slices. Place on a heated platter. Serve immediately.

Flank steak, often called London Broil, is one of the leanest cuts of beef. Because it has so little fat, it is a tough piece of meat. Slicing the prepared steak thinly on the diagonal produces a thin and more tender slice. It also allows for more servings while still satisfying the eye of the big-portion beef eaters.

Per Serving: Calories 314; Total Fat 14 g; Saturated Fat 6 g; Cholesterol 59 mg; Sodium 355 mg; Carbohydrate 7 g; Fiber 0 g; Protein 29 g; Calcium 35 mg
Nutritional profile includes the entire amount of the wine mixture.

Pan-Fried Cellophane Noodles with Spicy Beef

Wine: Chilean Cabernet Sauvignon   Makes 4 servings

2 tablespoons soy sauce
1 tablespoon chili sauce
1 tablespoon minced gingerroot
1 tablespoon minced garlic
1 (12-ounce) flank steak, thinly sliced
4 ounces cellophane noodles (dried mung bean threads)
1 tablespoon sesame oil
1 cup julienned zucchini
1 cup julienned yellow squash
1/2 cup julienned onion
1 large red bell pepper, chopped
1/2 cup oyster sauce

Method of preparation
▼ Combine the soy sauce, chili sauce, ginger, garlic and beef in a bowl, tossing to coat the beef well. Marinate in the refrigerator for 1 hour.
▼ Combine the noodles with hot water to cover in a bowl. Let stand for 30 minutes or until softened; drain well.
▼ Sauté the beef mixture in the sesame oil in a large sauté pan over high heat for 3 minutes or until light brown. Add the zucchini, yellow squash, onion and red pepper.
▼ Sauté for 3 to 4 minutes or just until the vegetables are tender-crisp. Stir in the noodles and oyster sauce gently.
▼ Cook until heated through. Serve immediately.

Sesame oil is a delightfully flavored oil and very little is needed to achieve the tantalizing aroma and taste of Asian cooking. Look for the darkest varieties, offered in most large supermarkets and gourmet shops. Sesame oil is a significant source of monounsaturated fatty acid, which most experts believe counters the cholesterol-raising effects of saturated fatty acids.

Per Serving: Calories 333; Total Fat 13 g; Saturated Fat 4 g; Cholesterol 44 mg; Sodium 1800 mg; Carbohydrate 37 g; Fiber 2 g; Protein 20 g; Calcium 39 mg

Spiced Charred Flank Steak with Roasted Garlic Aioli

Wine: California Cabernet Sauvignon   Makes 4 servings

For the aioli sauce
6 garlic cloves, sliced
1 teaspoon olive oil
1/4 cup nonfat mayonnaise
1 tablespoon chopped fresh chives
1 tablespoon lemon juice
Salt and pepper to taste

For the steak
1/4 teaspoon paprika
1/4 teaspoon garlic powder
1/4 teaspoon onion powder
Salt and pepper to taste
1 (16-ounce) flank steak

To prepare the aioli sauce
▼ Preheat the oven to 350 degrees.
▼ Combine the garlic with the olive oil in a baking pan. Bake for 10 to 12 minutes or until brown and tender.
▼ Mash the garlic with a fork in a bowl. Add the mayonnaise, chives, lemon juice, salt and pepper and mix well. Chill in the refrigerator.

To prepare the steak
▼ Combine the paprika, garlic powder, onion powder, salt and pepper in a small bowl. Rub into the steak and place in a shallow dish. Chill for 1 hour.
▼ Preheat the grill until the coals glow.
▼ Place the steak on the grill 5 to 6 inches above the coals. Grill for 5 to 6 minutes on each side for medium.

To assemble
▼ Place the steak on a cutting board and slice diagonally 1/4 inch thick. Place on a heated platter and top with the aioli sauce. Serve immediately.

Aioli is a garlic mayonnaise native to French cooking and often served with meats as well as fish and vegetables. It is typically made by crushing garlic and blending with egg yolk, olive oil, and lemon juice. By substituting nonfat mayonnaise for the egg yolk, the fat and cholesterol content drops significantly and reduces the risk of coming into contact with the salmonella bacteria.

Per Serving: Calories 236; Total Fat 13 g; Saturated Fat 5 g; Cholesterol 59 mg; Sodium 272 mg; Carbohydrate 5 g; Fiber 0 g; Protein 23 g; Calcium 16 mg

Braised Beef in Stout

Wine: French Bordeaux   Makes 4 servings

1¹/₂ pounds sirloin steak, trimmed, cubed
1 cup pearl onions
4 garlic cloves, minced
Salt and pepper to taste
2 cups low-sodium beef broth
2 cups chopped potatoes
1 (12-ounce) bottle stout
1 tablespoon brown sugar
¹/₂ teaspoon thyme
2 tablespoons flour
2 tablespoons red wine vinegar

Method of preparation
▼ Brown the beef in a nonstick pan over medium heat. Add the onions, garlic, salt and pepper and mix well.
▼ Sauté for 5 minutes. Stir in the broth, potatoes, stout, brown sugar and thyme. Bring to a boil; reduce heat.
▼ Simmer, covered, for 40 minutes or until the potatoes are tender, stirring occasionally. Stir in a mixture of the flour and wine vinegar. Season with salt and pepper.
▼ Cook just until heated through, stirring frequently. Spoon into heated bowls. Serve immediately.

▼ One way of avoiding the irritating eye burning and watering associated with cutting onions is to use pearl onions. Their small shape does away with the need to chop, and they add to the attractiveness of the dish as well. Onions are not particularly virtuous in terms of nutrition. However, they are a low-sodium flavoring agent when used fresh.

Per Serving: Calories 347; Total Fat 9 g; Saturated Fat 3 g; Cholesterol 104 mg; Sodium 466 mg; Carbohydrate 20 g; Fiber 2 g; Protein 44 g; Calcium 50 mg

Crispy Beef with Portobellos

Wine: Chilean Merlot   Makes 4 servings

1 fresh pineapple, peeled, chopped
1 pound sirloin steak, trimmed, thinly sliced
1 tablespoon hoisin sauce
1 tablespoon sugar
1 tablespoon cornstarch
2 teaspoons chili paste
1 teaspoon minced gingerroot
2 scallions, chopped
4 portobello mushrooms; stems removed
1 tablespoon sesame oil
Salt and pepper to taste

Method of preparation

▼ Process the pineapple in a food processor until puréed. Press the purée with a rubber spatula through a strainer into a bowl. Add the steak and mix well.
▼ Combine the hoisin sauce, sugar, cornstarch, chili paste, gingerroot and scallions in a bowl and mix well.
▼ Drain the steak, discarding the pineapple purée. Combine the steak and hoisin sauce mixture in a bowl, tossing to coat.
▼ Marinate at room temperature for 1 hour, tossing occasionally.
▼ Sauté the steak in a skillet over high heat until brown and crisp.
▼ Preheat the oven to 450 degrees.
▼ Brush the mushrooms with the sesame oil; sprinkle with salt and pepper. Arrange on a baking sheet.
▼ Roast for 5 to 6 minutes.
▼ Mound the steak on 4 heated plates; top each mound with mushrooms. Serve immediately.

This lean beef dish is made tender by the all-natural tenderizing action of papain, an enzyme found in fresh pineapple. Papain acts to break down the connective tissue that gives some cuts of meat a tough consistency. A perfect summer dish served with a cold crisp green salad.

Per Serving: Calories 412; Total Fat 11 g; Saturated Fat 3 g; Cholesterol 70 mg; Sodium 160 mg;
Carbohydrate 55 g; Fiber 6 g; Protein 27 g; Calcium 42 mg
Nutritional profile includes the entire amount of the pineapple purée.

Grilled Napoleon of Beef

Wine: California Merlot   Makes 4 servings

2 stalks lemon grass
1/2 cup chopped red onion
1/4 cup chopped red bell pepper
1 tablespoon vegetable oil
1 tablespoon lemon juice
1 teaspoon chili powder
1 teaspoon ginger
2 garlic cloves
1 1/2 pounds sirloin steak, trimmed
Salt and pepper to taste

Method of preparation
▼ Trim the lemon grass, using only the white base.
▼ Process the lemon grass base, red onion, red pepper, oil, lemon juice, chili powder, ginger and garlic in a food processor until of a paste consistency.
▼ Slice the steak crosswise into sixteen 1/4-inch thick strips. Spread the lemon grass mixture on each strip. Place in a dish.
▼ Marinate in the refrigerator for 8 to 10 hours.
▼ Preheat the grill.
▼ Thread the beef strips in a zigzag fashion on 4 skewers. Grill over hot coals for 6 to 7 minutes or until done to taste, turning frequently. Season with salt and pepper.
▼ Serve immediately.

The leanest cuts of beef include sirloin, eye-of-round, flank steak, and tenderloin. If you have shied away from beef for health reasons, reconsider beef recipes that utilize leaner cuts and modest portion sizes. Beef is one of the most abundant food sources of heme-iron, the form most readily absorbed by the body.

Per Serving: Calories 278; Total Fat 12 g; Saturated Fat 3 g; Cholesterol 104 mg; Sodium 106 mg; Carbohydrate 4 g; Fiber 1 g; Protein 37 g; Calcium 22 mg

Grilled Paradigm Burgers

Wine: French Merlot   Makes 4 servings

For the sauce

1/4 cup rice vinegar
1 tablespoon honey
1 tablespoon soy sauce
2 teaspoons hoisin sauce
1 garlic clove, minced

For the burgers

12 ounces extra-lean ground beef
1/2 cup fresh bread crumbs
1/4 cup minced scallions
2 tablespoons cold water
1 tablespoon minced fresh cilantro
2 teaspoons soy sauce
1 teaspoon wasabi powder
1 teaspoon grated gingerroot
1 teaspoon sugar
2 garlic cloves, minced

To prepare the sauce

▼ Combine the rice vinegar, honey, soy sauce, hoisin sauce and garlic in a bowl and mix well.

To prepare the burgers

▼ Preheat the grill.
▼ Combine the ground beef, bread crumbs, scallions, cold water, cilantro, soy sauce, wasabi powder, gingerroot, sugar and garlic in a bowl and mix well.
▼ Chill in the refrigerator for 20 minutes. Shape into 4 patties.
▼ Grill the patties 5 to 6 inches above hot coals for 5 to 6 minutes per side or until cooked through.

To assemble

▼ Arrange the burgers on a heated serving platter. Top each burger with the sauce.
▼ Serve immediately.

Break your burger paradigm by adding uncharacteristic seasonings and toppings. Wasabi powder, found in gourmet shops, is ground green horseradish root, which adds zip to ordinary ground meat. Prepared horseradish found in the refrigerated section of the supermarket makes for a suitable substitution.

Per Serving: Calories 245; Total Fat 15 g; Saturated Fat 6 g; Cholesterol 59 mg; Sodium 418 mg; Carbohydrate 10 g; Fiber 0 g; Protein 17 g; Calcium 24 mg

Braised Veal with
Aromatic Spices and Chiles

Wine: Chilean Cabernet Sauvignon   Makes 4 servings

2 cups low-sodium beef broth
4 poblano peppers, cut into 1/4-inch slices
2 garlic cloves
2 tablespoons balsamic vinegar
1/2 teaspoon curry powder
1/2 teaspoon cinnamon
1/4 teaspoon black pepper
1/4 teaspoon cumin
1 1/2 pounds veal cubes
1 tablespoon olive oil
1/2 cup finely ground gingersnaps

Method of preparation
▼ Preheat the oven to 325 degrees.
▼ Process the broth, poblano peppers, garlic, balsamic vinegar, curry powder, cinnamon, black pepper and cumin in a food processor until puréed.
▼ Brown the veal in the olive oil in a Dutch oven over medium heat. Spoon the poblano pepper mixture over the veal.
▼ Bake, covered, for 2 hours or until the veal is tender. Remove the veal to a heated serving platter.
▼ Bring the pan drippings to a boil. Whisk in the gingersnaps gradually. Cook until slightly thickened, whisking constantly; strain. Pour over the veal.
▼ Serve immediately.

Most cuts of veal are very lean. When purchasing, look for veal that is white or very pale pink color. If red in color, the veal is older and tougher. A comforting winter meal when served with confetti quinoa pilaf.

Per Serving: Calories 379; Total Fat 10 g; Saturated Fat 2 g; Cholesterol 143 mg; Sodium 574 mg; Carbohydrate 31 g; Fiber 1 g; Protein 43 g; Calcium 78 mg

Cumin Grilled Lamb Kabobs

Wine: Chianti   Makes 4 servings

2 tablespoons lime juice
1 teaspoon ground cumin
1 teaspoon coriander
$1/2$ teaspoon cinnamon
$1/2$ teaspoon nutmeg
$1/4$ teaspoon turmeric
$1/4$ teaspoon salt
4 garlic cloves, minced
$11/2$ pounds lamb, cubed
2 tablespoons garlic powder
1 tablespoon cumin seeds

Method of preparation
▼ Combine the lime juice, ground cumin, coriander, cinnamon, nutmeg, turmeric, salt and garlic in a bowl and mix well. Add the lamb, tossing to coat.
▼ Marinate, covered with plastic wrap, in the refrigerator for 8 to 10 hours, turning occasionally.
▼ Preheat the grill. Spray the cold grill rack with nonstick cooking spray. Sprinkle a mixture of the garlic powder and cumin seeds over the hot coals.
▼ Thread the lamb on metal skewers; do not crowd. Grill 5 inches above the coals for 10 to 12 minutes or until cooked through, turning frequently.
▼ Place the kabobs on a heated serving platter. Serve immediately.

Why is it that almost everyone has had an undesirable encounter with lamb? Perhaps more often than not this has been due to improper cooking or a past bad experience. Today's lamb is generally moist, flavorful, and lean. Almost any cut of lamb, including the leaner cuts of round, rump, and flank, may be cooked by dry heat methods such as grilling.

· Per Serving: Calories 259; Total Fat 10 g; Saturated Fat 3 g; Cholesterol 111 mg; Sodium 249 mg; Carbohydrate 6 g; Fiber 1 g; Protein 36 g; Calcium 48 mg

Lamb Vindaloo with Lentils

Wine: Chianti   Makes 4 servings

$1/2$ cup lentils
2 cups water
12 ounces lamb, cubed
3 tablespoons flour
1 tablespoon olive oil
$1/4$ cup chopped onion
2 garlic cloves, minced
2 cups chopped red tomatoes
$1/2$ cup sherry
$1/4$ cup chopped fresh parsley
1 tablespoon curry powder
1 teaspoon cumin
$1/4$ teaspoon turmeric
$1/4$ teaspoon cayenne
Salt and black pepper to taste
3 cups hot cooked rice

Method of preparation

▼ Sort and rinse the lentils. Combine with the water in a saucepan. Bring to a boil; reduce heat.
▼ Simmer, covered, for 35 minutes, stirring occasionally. Remove from heat; keep warm.
▼ Combine the lamb and flour in a sealable plastic bag, tossing to coat.
▼ Brown the lamb in the olive oil in a saucepan over medium heat. Remove the lamb to a platter. Add the onion and garlic to the pan drippings and mix well.
▼ Sauté for 5 minutes. Stir in the lamb, tomatoes, sherry, parsley, curry powder, cumin, turmeric, cayenne, salt and black pepper. Bring to a boil; reduce heat.
▼ Simmer for 30 minutes or until the lamb is tender, stirring occasionally. Stir in the undrained lentils.
▼ Spoon the rice onto a heated serving platter; top with the lamb.

No soaking required before cooking, inexpensive, and superior for protein content describes the lofty lentil! Lentils have the most protein of all the legumes, except soy beans. Most often available as brown or green, a red variety of lentils can also be obtained.

Per Serving: Calories 521; Total Fat 9 g; Saturated Fat 2 g; Cholesterol 55 mg; Sodium 127 mg; Carbohydrate 70 g; Fiber 10 g; Protein 31 g; Calcium 120 mg

Mediterranean Lamb Stew

Wine: Chianti   Makes 4 servings

1¹/2 pounds lamb, cut into 1-inch cubes
¹/4 cup flour
Salt and pepper to taste
1 tablespoon olive oil
¹/2 teaspoon coriander
¹/4 teaspoon chopped fresh thyme
¹/4 teaspoon chopped fresh rosemary
1 garlic clove, minced
2 cups low-sodium beef broth
1 cup red wine
1 cup chopped tomato
24 small white onions, blanched
¹/2 cup black olives

Method of preparation
▼ Coat the lamb with a mixture of the flour, salt and pepper.
▼ Brown the lamb in the olive oil in a skillet over medium heat. Sprinkle with the coriander, thyme, rosemary and garlic. Add the broth, red wine, tomato, salt and pepper and mix well.
▼ Simmer over medium heat for 1 hour, stirring occasionally. Stir in the onions and olives.
▼ Simmer for 30 minutes longer, stirring occasionally. Serve immediately.

Although the health community does debate over the need to restrict salt in the average person's diet, most of us could certainly do with less. As one ages, taste sensations dull and the use of the salt shaker and high-sodium processed foods tends to increase. Instead of salt, consider wine as a flavor enhancer. Some of the compounds in wine mimic the taste of salt.

Per Serving: Calories 382; Total Fat 14 g; Saturated Fat 4 g; Cholesterol 111 mg; Sodium 799 mg; Carbohydrate 14 g; Fiber 2 g; Protein 42 g; Calcium 81 mg

Porter Ale-Braised Loin of Pork

Wine: Riesling   Makes 4 servings

1¹/₄ pounds boneless pork sirloin
2 cups chopped onions
1 cup chopped carrot
12 ounces dark porter ale
1 garlic clove, minced
2 bay leaves
Salt and pepper to taste

Method of preparation
▼ Preheat the oven to 350 degrees.
▼ Brown the pork on all sides in a Dutch oven. Remove the pork to a platter. Add the onions and carrot to the pan drippings and mix well.
▼ Sauté for 5 minutes or until brown. Stir in the pork, ale, garlic, bay leaves, salt and pepper. Bring to a boil.
▼ Bake, covered, for 2 hours or until the pork is tender. Discard the bay leaves. Remove the pork to a cutting board.
▼ Cut into ¹/₄-inch slices. Place on a heated serving platter.
▼ Process the vegetables and pan drippings in a food processor until puréed. Pour over the pork.
▼ Serve immediately.

The ale makes this dish! If you're concerned about the alcohol, it boils out at approximately 175 degrees, while water boils at 212 degrees. The flavor of the beef is left while the alcohol disappears. Brown rice pilaf makes a nice accompaniment to this dish.

Per Serving: Calories 334; Total Fat 12 g; Saturated Fat 4 g; Cholesterol 115 mg; Sodium 378 mg; Carbohydrate 10 g; Fiber 2 g; Protein 39 g; Calcium 75 mg

Roasted Peppered Pork Tenderloin

Wine: Pinot Blanc   Makes 4 servings

1 tablespoon olive oil
1 tablespoon chopped fresh rosemary
2 teaspoons peppercorn mélange, crushed
Juice of 1 lemon
2 garlic cloves, minced
1¹/₂ pounds pork tenderloin, trimmed

Method of preparation
▼ Pour a mixture of the olive oil, rosemary, peppercorns, lemon juice and garlic over
  the pork in a deep dish, turning to coat.
▼ Marinate in the refrigerator for 30 minutes, turning several times.
▼ Preheat the oven to 375 degrees.
▼ Brown the tenderloin in a skillet on all sides. Place in a roasting pan.
▼ Roast for 45 minutes or until a meat thermometer registers 155 degrees.
▼ Let stand for 10 minutes before slicing.

Pepper used for seasoning is at its peak when freshly ground. Mélange or
mixture of peppercorns can be found in cooking stores or gourmet shops.
Usually three or four different colored varieties are combined, which adds to the
visual quality of your final product.

Per Serving: Calories 447; Total Fat 15 g; Saturated Fat 5 g; Cholesterol 221 mg; Sodium 171 mg;
Carbohydrate 4 g; Fiber 0 g; Protein 72 g; Calcium 39 mg

Thai Braised Stuffed Tenderloin of Pork

Wine: Gewürztraminer   Makes 4 servings

For the tenderloin

1¼ pounds pork tenderloin
¼ cup bulgur
1 red bell pepper, seeded
3 scallions
1 piece gingerroot
1 carrot
2 egg whites
1 tablespoon sesame oil
1 tablespoon soy sauce
½ teaspoon five-spice powder

For the sauce

2 cups chicken stock
¼ cup hoisin sauce
2 tablespoons minced gingerroot
2 teaspoons curry paste

To prepare the tenderloin

▼ Preheat the oven to 350 degrees.
▼ Trim the pork. Cut approximately 4 ounces from the narrow end and coarsely chop, reserving the remaining tenderloin.
▼ Combine 4 ounces pork, bulgur, red pepper, scallions, gingerroot, carrot, egg whites, sesame oil, soy sauce and five-spice powder in a food processor container fitted with a steel blade. Pulse until finely chopped.
▼ Butterfly the reserved tenderloin. Pound ⅛ inch thick between sheets of plastic wrap with a meat mallet. Spread with the pork mixture and roll as for a jelly roll to enclose the filling. Wrap in heavy-duty plastic wrap, then in foil. Place on a baking sheet.
▼ Roast for 30 to 35 minutes or until a meat thermometer registers 155 degrees.

To prepare the sauce

▼ Combine the stock, hoisin sauce, gingerroot and curry paste in a saucepan. Bring to a boil; reduce heat.
▼ Simmer until reduced by ½, stirring frequently. Keep warm.

To assemble

▼ Unwrap the tenderloin and cut diagonally into slices.
▼ Arrange the tenderloin on a heated serving platter; drizzle with the warm sauce.
▼ Serve immediately.

Hoisin sauce is sometimes referred to as "Chinese Barbeque Sauce" but the flavor is much more tantalizing than the American version. A combination of sugar, vinegar, soy bean paste, salt, garlic, and flavorings, the sodium content can be quite high. The sauce is available in supermarkets, but you will more likely find a better-quality product in an Asian market or gourmet food store.

Per Serving: Calories 486; Total Fat 17 g; Saturated Fat 5 g; Cholesterol 187 mg; Sodium 463 mg; Carbohydrate 17 g; Fiber 3 g; Protein 64 g; Calcium 40 mg

Balsamic Braised Pork Tenderloin with Fine Herbs

Wine: Chilean Merlot   Makes 4 servings

1 1/2 pounds pork tenderloin, trimmed
1/2 cup flour
1/2 teaspoon salt
1/4 teaspoon pepper
1 tablespoon olive oil
2 tablespoons minced shallots
2 garlic cloves, minced
2/3 cup balsamic vinegar
1/4 cup chicken stock
1 tablespoon chopped fresh sage
1 tablespoon chopped fresh rosemary
1 tablespoon chopped fresh thyme

Method of preparation
▼ Coat the tenderloin with a mixture of the flour, salt and pepper.
▼ Brown the tenderloin on both sides in the olive oil in a nonstick saucepan over medium heat. Remove the pork to a platter.
▼ Stir the shallots and garlic into the pan drippings. Sauté for 2 to 3 minutes. Add the balsamic vinegar and stock and mix well.
▼ Simmer for 2 to 3 minutes, stirring frequently. Return the tenderloin to the saucepan.
▼ Simmer, covered, for 20 to 25 minutes or until a meat thermometer registers 155 degrees, basting with pan drippings frequently. Remove the tenderloin to a platter.
▼ Add the sage, rosemary and thyme to the pan drippings and mix well. Cook until reduced by 1/2, stirring constantly.
▼ Cut the tenderloin into 1-inch slices. Arrange on a heated serving platter and drizzle with the herb mixture. Serve immediately.

Balsamic vinegar, an aged Italian wine vinegar, should be a staple in every kitchen. Its unusual flavor is difficult to describe and never to be forgotten. The balsamic vinegar, chicken stock, and herb mixture combines to make a virtually fat-free cooking medium that imparts taste without extra calories from fat.

Per Serving: Calories 511; Total Fat 15 g; Saturated Fat 5 g; Cholesterol 221 mg; Sodium 438 mg; Carbohydrate 16 g; Fiber 0 g; Protein 74 g; Calcium 35 mg

Spezzatino di Maiale

Wine: Pinot Blanc   Makes 4 servings

1 pound pork tenderloin, cut into thin strips
1 tablespoon olive oil
2 elephant garlic cloves, minced
3 scallions, chopped
3 plum tomatoes, peeled, seeded, chopped
1 1/2 cups cooked white beans
2 cups escarole, cooked
1/2 cup chicken stock
3 tablespoons minced fresh basil
2 tablespoons pine nuts
1 tablespoon minced fresh parsley
Salt and pepper to taste

Method of preparation

▼ Brown the pork in the olive oil in a saucepan over medium heat. Remove the pork to a platter. Stir the garlic into the pan drippings.
▼ Sauté for 2 minutes. Add the scallions and tomatoes and mix well.
▼ Simmer for 3 to 4 minutes, stirring frequently. Stir in the white beans, escarole, stock, basil, pine nuts and parsley.
▼ Simmer until slightly thickened, stirring frequently. Add the pork, salt and pepper and mix well. Serve immediately.

   You can eat pork on a low-fat diet! Fresh pork cuts of the 1990s contain an average of 31 percent less fat than reported in the early 1980s. Look for loin cuts when choosing pork. Ribs and chops will contain a higher percentage of fat.

Per Serving: Calories 452; Total Fat 14 g; Saturated Fat 4 g; Cholesterol 147 mg; Sodium 134 mg; Carbohydrate 24 g; Fiber 6 g; Protein 57 g; Calcium 106 mg

Vegetable Pork Stew with Miso and Ginger

Wine: Alsatian Gentil   Makes 4 servings

12 ounces pork tenderloin, trimmed, cut into 1-inch cubes
1 tablespoon olive oil
1 cup julienned onion
1 cup julienned carrot
1 cup julienned turnips
1 cup chicken stock
2 tablespoons red miso
1 tablespoon minced gingerroot
Salt and pepper to taste
12 ounces daikon, peeled, sliced, julienned
8 ounces tofu, cut into 1/2-inch cubes
1/4 cup chopped scallions

Method of preparation

▼ Brown the tenderloin in the olive oil in a saucepan over medium heat. Remove the tenderloin to a platter.
▼ Stir the onion, carrot and turnips into the pan drippings. Sauté for 2 to 3 minutes. Add the stock and pork and mix well.
▼ Simmer, covered, for 25 minutes, stirring occasionally. Stir in the miso, gingerroot, salt and pepper.
▼ Simmer until the liquid is reduced by 1/2, stirring frequently. Sprinkle with the daikon, tofu and scallions.
▼ Serve immediately.

Miso is a soybean paste that is made by fermenting soybeans, rice, salt, and water. Found in any Asian market or gourmet store, it is available in two varieties: light, or dark and red. Try substituting miso in recipes where you use soy sauce, but use sparingly since it is very salty.

Per Serving: Calories 342; Total Fat 13 g; Saturated Fat 3 g; Cholesterol 110 mg; Sodium 602 mg;
Carbohydrate 14 g; Fiber 5 g; Protein 43 g; Calcium 137 mg

Ballotine of Baby Chicken

Wine: French Chardonnay   Makes 4 servings

For the stuffing

$1/2$ cup fresh crab meat
$1/4$ cup minced cucumber
$1/4$ cup dry white wine
$1/2$ teaspoon minced gingerroot
$1/4$ cup chopped tomato
1 teaspoon chopped fresh rosemary
4 chicken quarters

For the sauce

$1^1/2$ cups chopped tomatoes
$1/2$ cup dry white wine
2 tablespoons chopped fresh basil
2 teaspoons minced shallots
$1/2$ cup evaporated skim milk
1 tablespoon lemon juice
1 tablespoon butter
Salt and pepper to taste
2 tablespoons julienned fresh basil

To prepare the stuffing

▼ Simmer the crab meat, cucumber, white wine and gingerroot in a saucepan for 2 minutes, stirring frequently. Drain, reserving the liquid. Stir in the tomato and rosemary.
▼ Preheat the oven to 350 degrees.
▼ Rinse the chicken and pat dry. Skin and bone the chicken.
▼ Stuff the thigh section with the stuffing and secure with wooden picks. Place in a baking pan.
▼ Bake for 1 hour or until a meat thermometer registers 165 degrees.

To prepare the sauce

▼ Combine the reserved liquid, tomatoes, white wine, chopped basil and shallots in a saucepan and mix well.
▼ Simmer for 20 minutes, stirring frequently. Process in a food processor until puréed; strain. Return to the saucepan. Stir in the evaporated skim milk.
▼ Simmer until slightly thickened, stirring constantly. Whisk in the lemon juice, butter, salt and pepper until blended. Stir in the julienned basil.

To assemble

▼ Spoon $1/4$ cup of the sauce onto each of 4 heated dinner plates; top with the chicken. Serve immediately.

There's more to chicken than the chicken breast alone! This recipe utilizes skinned chicken quarters. Although a little higher in fat, the dark meat of chicken is more moist and provides more iron than breast meat. Cook all poultry to an internal temperature of 165 degrees.

Per Serving: Calories 459; Total Fat 14 g; Saturated Fat 5 g; Cholesterol 255 mg; Sodium 372 mg; Carbohydrate 8 g; Fiber 1 g; Protein 64 g; Calcium 152 mg

Breast of Chicken with Citrus Cream

Wine: Pinot Grigio   Makes 4 servings

1 1/2 pounds boneless skinless chicken breast halves
1/2 cup currants
1/2 cup water
2 tablespoons brandy
2 tablespoons olive oil
2 tablespoons minced shallots
1 cup evaporated skim milk
1/2 cup chicken stock
1 tablespoon chopped fresh thyme
1 teaspoon chopped fresh rosemary
Sections of 2 medium ruby red grapefruits
Salt and pepper to taste

Method of preparation
▼ Rinse the chicken and pat dry.
▼ Combine the currants and water in a saucepan. Bring to a boil; reduce heat.
▼ Simmer for 3 minutes; drain. Add the brandy and mix well.
▼ Sauté the chicken in the olive oil in a skillet over medium heat for 3 to 4 minutes on each side. Remove the chicken to a platter.
▼ Sauté the shallots in the pan drippings for 2 minutes or until tender. Add the currant mixture, evaporated skim milk and stock and mix well.
▼ Cook until reduced by 1/2, stirring constantly. Return the chicken to the skillet.
▼ Simmer for 30 to 40 minutes or until the chicken is cooked through, stirring occasionally. Sprinkle with the thyme and rosemary.
▼ Cook for 3 to 4 minutes longer, stirring frequently. Stir in the grapefruit sections; season with salt and pepper.
▼ Remove the chicken to a heated serving platter; top with the grapefruit sauce. Serve immediately.

You have just saved 272 calories, 45 grams of fat, and added a significant amount of bone-building calcium to this recipe by using evaporated skim milk instead of light cream! Small amounts of cream may be used in lower-fat entrées. However, since this selection calls for a large volume of liquid for the sauce, you will manage the nutritional content better by switching to similar-consistency evaporated skim milk.

Per Serving: Calories 453; Total Fat 10 g; Saturated Fat 2 g; Cholesterol 101 mg; Sodium 192 mg; Carbohydrate 41 g; Fiber 4 g; Protein 47 g; Calcium 255 mg

Breast of Chicken Cacciatore Contemporary-Style

Wine: Italian Orvieto   Makes 4 servings

For the sauce

1 cup (1/4-inch pieces) red tomatoes
1 cup (1/4-inch pieces) yellow tomatoes
3 tablespoons chopped fresh basil
2 tablespoons chopped Italian parsley
1/4 teaspoon red pepper flakes
Salt and black pepper to taste

For the chicken

1 1/2 pounds boneless skinless chicken
   breast halves
Salt and pepper to taste
1 red bell pepper, julienned
1 yellow bell pepper, thinly sliced
2 portobello mushrooms, thinly sliced
4 scallions, thinly sliced
1 tablespoon olive oil
1/4 cup chopped fresh basil
2 garlic cloves, minced

To prepare the sauce

▼ Combine the tomatoes, basil, Italian parsley, red pepper flakes, salt and black pepper in a bowl and mix well.
▼ Chill, covered, in the refrigerator for 2 hours.

To prepare the chicken

▼ Rinse the chicken and pat dry. Pound the chicken between sheets of waxed paper with a meat mallet until slightly flattened. Season with salt and pepper.
▼ Sauté the bell peppers, mushrooms and scallions in the olive oil in a saucepan over medium heat for 2 minutes. Stir in the basil and garlic.
▼ Sauté for 1 minute.
▼ Spoon the filling in the center of each chicken breast; roll as for an egg roll to enclose the filling. Wrap each chicken breast in plastic wrap and then in foil.
▼ Place the chicken rolls in a pan of simmering water. Simmer for 20 minutes or until the chicken is cooked through.

To assemble

▼ Slice the chicken diagonally into 1-inch slices.
▼ Spread 4 ounces of the sauce on each of 4 dinner plates. Arrange the sliced chicken around the outer edge of the plates.

This chicken recipe certainly breaks the paradigm of traditional cacciatore since its presentation is really "inside-out"! Also, no one will even realize that they are eating two full vegetable servings as part of the entrée. The National Cancer Institute suggests five fruits and/or vegetables be a part of one's diet on a daily basis.

Per Serving: Calories 274; Total Fat 7 g; Saturated Fat 1 g; Cholesterol 99 mg; Sodium 131 mg; Carbohydrate 11 g; Fiber 2 g; Protein 42 g; Calcium 59 mg

Fricassee of Chicken Andaluzas

Wine: Pinot Grigio   Makes 4 servings

4 (5-ounce) boneless skinless chicken breast halves
1/2 cup pitted prunes
5 garlic cloves
2 tablespoons vinegar
1 tablespoon olive oil
1 teaspoon oregano
1 tablespoon olive oil
1/4 cup julienned red bell pepper
1/4 cup julienned green bell pepper
1/4 cup julienned onion
1/2 cup sherry
1/4 cup sliced olives
1 tablespoon lime juice
Salt and pepper to taste
1/4 cup chopped fresh parsley

Method of preparation

▼ Rinse the chicken and pat dry. Place in a dish.
▼ Process the prunes, garlic, vinegar, 1 tablespoon olive oil and oregano in a food processor until puréed. Brush both sides of the chicken with the prune purée; reserve the remaining prune purée.
▼ Chill for 30 minutes.
▼ Sauté the chicken in 1 tablespoon olive oil in a skillet over medium heat for 2 minutes on each side. Remove the chicken to a platter. Add the bell peppers and onion and mix well.
▼ Sauté for 2 minutes. Stir in the sherry, olives and lime juice.
▼ Cook for 1 minute or longer, stirring frequently. Return the chicken and reserved prune purée to the skillet.
▼ Simmer, covered, for 20 to 25 minutes, stirring occasionally; do not overcook. Season with salt and pepper.
▼ Spoon onto a heated serving platter; sprinkle with the parsley. Serve immediately.

Prunes, underutilized in cooking, should command much more respect due to their sweet taste and fiber content. Not just any plum is destined to be a prune. Plums must be sufficiently high in sugar content and firm enough to permit drying without fermentation around the pit. As with all dried fruit, calories can add up quickly so use them judiciously.

Per Serving: Calories 280; Total Fat 10 g; Saturated Fat 1 g; Cholesterol 51 mg; Sodium 198 mg;
Carbohydrate 20 g; Fiber 2 g; Protein 22 g; Calcium 106 mg

Grilled Asian Chicken

Wine: Alsatian Gentil   Makes 4 servings

For the chicken

1 pound boneless skinless chicken breast
   halves
1/4 cup soy sauce
1 tablespoon sesame oil
4 garlic cloves, minced

For the vegetables

4 ounces mung bean threads
1 1/2 cups julienned romaine
1 red bell pepper, julienned
1/2 cup julienned carrot

For the sauce

1/4 cup minced fresh mint
2 tablespoons sesame oil
1 tablespoon rice vinegar
1 tablespoon lime juice
1 tablespoon chili paste
1 tablespoon sugar

To prepare the chicken
▼ Rinse the chicken and pat dry. Combine the chicken with a mixture of the soy sauce, sesame oil and garlic in a bowl, turning to coat.
▼ Marinate in the refrigerator for 2 hours, turning occasionally.
▼ Preheat the grill.
▼ Drain the chicken, discarding the marinade.
▼ Grill over medium-hot coals for 6 minutes per side or until cooked through.

To prepare the vegetables
▼ Soak the mung bean threads in enough hot water to cover in a bowl until softened; drain.
▼ Combine with the romaine, red pepper and carrot in a bowl and toss gently.

To prepare the sauce
▼ Combine the mint, sesame oil, rice vinegar, lime juice, chili paste and sugar in a bowl and mix well.

To assemble
▼ Cut the chicken into thin strips. Add to the vegetable mixture and toss gently. Stir in the sauce.
▼ Spoon onto chilled dinner plates. Serve immediately.

Perfect for a light meal on a hot summer night, this low-calorie salad is high in flavor and satisfaction. The mung bean threads are actually Oriental pasta made from mung bean flour. All mung bean products are available in gourmet stores and Asian markets.

Per Serving: Calories 361; Total Fat 12 g; Saturated Fat 2 g; Cholesterol 66 mg; Sodium 1043 mg;
Carbohydrate 35 g; Fiber 2 g; Protein 28 g; Calcium 38 mg
The nutritional profile includes the entire amount of the marinade.

Grilled Chicken with Basil Gremolata

Wine: Italian Vernaccia   Makes 4 servings

For the gremolata

1/4 cup minced red bell pepper
1 tablespoon minced fresh basil
2 garlic cloves, minced
1 teaspoon minced lime zest

For the chicken

4 (6-ounce) boneless skinless chicken
  breast halves
1/4 cup lime juice
2 tablespoons olive oil
1 teaspoon pepper

To prepare the gremolata
▼ Combine the red pepper, basil, garlic and lime zest in a bowl and mix well.

To prepare the chicken
▼ Preheat the grill. Spray the grill rack with nonstick cooking spray.
▼ Rinse the chicken and pat dry. Pound 1/4 inch thick between sheets of plastic wrap with a meat mallet.
▼ Pour a mixture of the lime juice, olive oil and pepper over the chicken in a glass dish, turning to coat.
▼ Marinate in the refrigerator for 30 minutes. Drain the chicken, reserving the marinade.
▼ Grill 5 to 6 inches above the heat over hot coals for 3 to 4 minutes on each side or until cooked through, basting with the reserved marinade frequently.

To assemble
▼ Arrange the chicken on a heated serving platter. Sprinkle with the gremolata. Serve immediately.

Gremolata is a mixture of seasonings usually used for sauces and pan gravies. Sauces are often omitted from healthy fare because of the extra fat and salt they contain. The difficulty with omitting sauces from a recipe is that they are often a significant part of the flavor of the dish. The gremolata utilized here is fat-free and salt-free, again breaking the paradigm for sauces.

Per Serving: Calories 263; Total Fat 10 g; Saturated Fat 2 g; Cholesterol 99 mg; Sodium 117 mg;
Carbohydrate 3 g; Fiber 0 g; Protein 40 g; Calcium 29 mg

Oven-Roasted Chicken Paillards with Belgian Endive

Wine: French Pouilly-Fuissé   Makes 4 servings

4 (6-ounce) boneless skinless chicken breast halves
Salt and pepper to taste
2 tablespoons lemon juice
1 tablespoon olive oil
8 large sage leaves, chopped
3 ounces Vermont Cheddar cheese, shredded
2 heads Belgian endive, separated into spears

Method of preparation
▼ Preheat the oven to 400 degrees.
▼ Rinse the chicken and pat dry. Pound $1/8$ inch thick between sheets of plastic wrap with a meat mallet. Season the chicken with salt and pepper.
▼ Combine the lemon juice and olive oil in a bowl and mix well. Drizzle the chicken with $1/2$ of the lemon juice mixture; rub with the sage. Place on a baking sheet.
▼ Bake for 6 to 7 minutes; turn. Sprinkle the cheese over the chicken.
▼ Arrange the endive on a baking sheet. Drizzle with the remaining lemon juice mixture.
▼ Bake the chicken and endive for 6 to 7 minutes or until the chicken is cooked through.
▼ Arrange the endive stem side in on a serving platter. Top with the chicken. Serve immediately.

Endive, a small cigar-shaped plant, is slightly bitter to the taste and lends itself to an attractive presentation. Maintain freshness by wrapping the endive in plastic wrap, storing in the refrigerator, and using within a couple of days after purchasing. Endive is a significant source of vitamin A and folate.

Per Serving: Calories 335; Total Fat 14 g; Saturated Fat 6 g; Cholesterol 121 mg; Sodium 263 mg;
Carbohydrate 6 g; Fiber 3 g; Protein 46 g; Calcium 275 mg

Roasted Chicken Margarita

Wine: Alsatian Pinot Blanc   Makes 4 servings

4 (6-ounce) boneless skinless chicken breast halves
3 teaspoons olive oil
2 teaspoons flour
1/2 cup chicken stock
2 tablespoons Cointreau
1 1/2 tablespoons lime juice
1 tablespoon tequila
1/2 teaspoon lime zest

Method of preparation
▼ Preheat the oven to 350 degrees.
▼ Rinse the chicken and pat dry. Pound 1/4 inch thick between sheets of plastic wrap with a meat mallet.
▼ Sauté 2 of the chicken breasts in 1 teaspoon of the olive oil in an ovenproof skillet over medium heat for 2 minutes per side. Remove the chicken to a platter. Add 1 more teaspoon of the olive oil to the skillet. Repeat the process with the remaining chicken breasts.
▼ Add the remaining olive oil to the pan drippings in the skillet and mix well. Stir in the flour.
▼ Cook for 1 minute, stirring constantly. Add the stock gradually, whisking until blended. Stir in the Cointreau, lime juice and tequila.
▼ Cook for 1 minute, stirring constantly. Return the chicken to the skillet, turning to coat.
▼ Bake for 10 to 12 minutes or until the chicken is cooked through.
▼ Arrange the chicken on a heated serving platter; drizzle with the sauce. Sprinkle with the lime zest.
▼ Serve immediately.

The combination of Cointreau, lime juice, and tequila brings a South-of-the-Border flair to the ordinary yet versatile chicken breast. The chicken breast is hard to ignore when planning healthy meals. A six-ounce portion of chicken contains a modest 194 calories, 3 grams of fat, and 99 milligrams of cholesterol.

Per Serving: Calories 262; Total Fat 6 g; Saturated Fat 1 g; Cholesterol 99 mg; Sodium 116 mg; Carbohydrate 4 g; Fiber 0 g; Protein 40 g; Calcium 22 mg

Savory Pan-Roasted Chicken

Wine: California Meursault   Makes 4 servings

1 1/2 pounds boneless skinless chicken breast halves
1 tablespoon olive oil
1 cup thinly sliced onion
1/2 cup white wine
1/2 cup chicken stock
20 garlic cloves
2 bay leaves
2 cinnamon sticks
1 tablespoon thyme
1/2 teaspoon cayenne
3 tablespoons grated Parmesan cheese

Method of preparation
▼ Rinse the chicken and pat dry.
▼ Sauté the chicken in the olive oil in a skillet over medium heat for 3 to 4 minutes per side. Add the onion and mix well.
▼ Sauté for 2 minutes. Stir in the white wine, stock, garlic, bay leaves, cinnamon sticks, thyme and cayenne.
▼ Simmer, covered, for 20 to 25 minutes or until the chicken is cooked through, stirring occasionally. Remove the chicken with a slotted spoon to a heated serving platter.
▼ Cook the remaining sauce for 3 to 4 minutes or until reduced by 1/2, stirring frequently. Discard the bay leaves and cinnamon sticks. Pour over the chicken; sprinkle with the cheese.
▼ Serve immediately.

Even a small amount of olive oil contributes substantial flavor to a dish. Produced mainly in Italy, Greece, and Spain, this monounsaturated cholesterol-lowering oil is available in a variety of grades. The most flavorful is the extra-virgin variety, which is pressed cold from fresh ripe olives. Be aware though . . . a fat is a fat! Use sparingly, as one tablespoon of most any oil weighs in at 14 grams of fat and 120 calories.

Per Serving: Calories 316; Total Fat 8 g; Saturated Fat 2 g; Cholesterol 102 mg; Sodium 341 mg; Carbohydrate 14 g; Fiber 5 g; Protein 43 g; Calcium 232 mg

Supreme of Chicken
with Chiffonade of Vegetables

Wine: French Mercurey Blanc   Makes 4 servings

1¹/2 pounds boneless skinless chicken breast halves
2 tablespoons minced shallots
3 tablespoons butter
1 teaspoon chopped fresh thyme
1 cup julienned leeks
¹/2 cup julienned carrot
¹/2 cup julienned red bell pepper
1 cup chicken stock

Method of preparation

▼ Preheat the oven to 350 degrees.
▼ Rinse the chicken and pat dry. Arrange in a baking pan.
▼ Sauté the shallots in 2 tablespoons of the butter in a saucepan over medium heat for 3 minutes. Stir in the thyme.
▼ Sauté for 1 minute. Pour over the chicken, turning to coat.
▼ Bake for 25 minutes or until the chicken is tender.
▼ Add the remaining 1 tablespoon butter to the saucepan. Stir in the leeks, carrot and red pepper.
▼ Sauté for 2 to 3 minutes. Add the stock and mix well.
▼ Simmer for 5 minutes, stirring frequently.
▼ Arrange the chicken on a heated serving platter; top with the chiffonade of vegetables.

Resembling an overgrown scallion, the leek is actually a mild-tasting relative of the onion. Leeks are most noted for their contribution to vichyssoise, a cold puréed potato and leek soup, but are very versatile and lend themselves to a variety of dishes. Choose young small plants with crisp dark green tops, as they are more tender and tastier than larger bulbs.

Per Serving: Calories 315; Total Fat 12 g; Saturated Fat 6 g; Cholesterol 122 mg; Sodium 213 mg; Carbohydrate 10 g; Fiber 2 g; Protein 41 g; Calcium 62 mg

Breast of Chicken en Papillote

Wine: French Pouilly-Fuissé   Makes 4 servings

1¹/2 pounds boneless skinless chicken breasts, sliced
2 tablespoons sake
1 tablespoon soy sauce
1 tablespoon oyster sauce
¹/2 teaspoon sugar
2 cups sliced shiitake mushrooms
1 cup sliced scallions
¹/2 cup julienned carrot
2 tablespoons grated gingerroot
1 tablespoon vegetable oil

Method of preparation

▼ Preheat the oven to 350 degrees.
▼ Rinse the chicken and pat dry.
▼ Combine the sake, soy sauce, oyster sauce and sugar in a bowl and mix well. Add the chicken, turning to coat.
▼ Marinate in the refrigerator for 1 hour.
▼ Combine the mushrooms, scallions, carrot, gingerroot and oil in a bowl and mix well.
▼ Lay four 12x12-inch sheets of parchment paper on a flat surface; cut each sheet into a heart shape.
▼ Drain the chicken, discarding the marinade. Arrange 6 ounces of chicken on 1 side of a heart; spoon ¹/4 of the mushroom mixture on the chicken. Fold 1 side of the heart over the filling to form ¹/2 of a heart; fold the edge to seal. Place on a baking sheet. Repeat the process with the remaining hearts.
▼ Bake for 25 minutes; the parchment paper will puff like a balloon. Serve in the paper.

The enjoyment of a meal involves more than just the taste of the food. This recipe emphasizes the role of the food's aroma. Cooking in parchment, or en papillote, is a method for keeping low-fat dishes moist and delicate. When cooking, the moisture in the parchment wrapping evaporates causing the paper to puff. When completed, the parchment paper is cut and the aromas burst into the air.

Per Serving: Calories 371; Total Fat 7 g; Saturated Fat 1 g; Cholesterol 99 mg; Sodium 494 mg;
Carbohydrate 34 g; Fiber 6 g; Protein 44 g; Calcium 51 mg
The nutritional profile includes the entire amount of the marinade.

Macédoine of Chicken with Julienned Vegetables and Brown Rice

Wine: Chilean Chardonnay   Makes 4 servings

For the sauce

1/4 cup fresh lemon juice
2 tablespoons olive oil
1 garlic clove, minced
1/4 teaspoon finely chopped fresh
    oregano
1/4 teaspoon finely chopped fresh basil
Salt and pepper to taste

For the macédoine

1 pound boneless skinless chicken
    breasts, julienned
3/4 cup uncooked brown rice
1 egg, beaten
2 cups chicken stock
1/2 cup julienned carrot
1/2 cup julienned celery
1/2 cup julienned scallions
1/2 cup julienned peeled tomato
1/4 cup chopped fresh parsley
Salt and pepper to taste

To prepare the sauce

▼ Combine the lemon juice, olive oil, garlic, oregano, basil, salt and pepper in a bowl and mix well.

To prepare the macédoine

▼ Preheat the oven to 350 degrees.
▼ Rinse the chicken and pat dry.
▼ Combine the brown rice and egg in an ovenproof pan and mix well.
▼ Cook over medium heat until the rice is dry and the grains separate, stirring constantly. Stir in the chicken, stock, carrot, celery, scallions, tomato, parsley, salt and pepper.
▼ Bake, covered, for 35 to 40 minutes or until the liquid is absorbed. Fluff with a fork; do not stir.

To assemble

▼ Spoon the macédoine of chicken onto a heated serving platter; drizzle with the sauce. Serve immediately.

Since brown rice retains both the bran and the germ of the rice kernel, it has more fiber and vitamin E than white rice. Nutlike in flavor and a bit chewier than white rice, brown rice has a cooking time that is somewhat longer and more liquid is required. If not used within a month of purchase, store in the refrigerator to delay its oils becoming rancid.

Per Serving: Calories 363; Total Fat 11 g; Saturated Fat 2 g; Cholesterol 119 mg; Sodium 119 mg; Carbohydrate 33 g; Fiber 2 g; Protein 32 g; Calcium 61 mg

New Wave Chicken and Mushroom Stroganoff

Wine: Australian Chardonnay   Makes 4 servings

12 ounces boneless skinless chicken breast halves, cut into strips
1/2 cup low-fat cottage cheese
1/2 cup light sour cream
1/4 cup Marsala
2 tablespoons Dijon mustard
2 teaspoons olive oil
2 garlic cloves, minced
1/4 teaspoon red pepper flakes
1 cup sliced carrot
1/2 cup sliced red onion
3 cups sliced shiitake mushrooms
2 tablespoons water
2 tablespoons soy sauce
3 cups hot cooked egg noodles

Method of preparation
▼ Rinse the chicken and pat dry.
▼ Process the cottage cheese, sour cream, Marsala and Dijon mustard in a food processor for 1 minute or until puréed.
▼ Heat 1 teaspoon of the olive oil in a large skillet over medium heat until hot. Add the chicken.
▼ Sauté for 5 minutes. Transfer the chicken to a platter. Heat the remaining 1 teaspoon olive oil in the skillet over medium heat until hot. Stir in the garlic and red pepper flakes.
▼ Sauté for 1 minute. Add the carrot, red onion and mushrooms; mix well.
▼ Sauté for 5 minutes. Return the chicken to the skillet. Stir in the water and soy sauce.
▼ Cook, covered, for 5 minutes, stirring occasionally. Remove from heat. Stir in the cottage cheese purée gently.
▼ Spoon the hot noodles onto a heated serving platter; top with the chicken and mushroom mixture. Serve immediately.

Stroganoff is typically made with whipping cream or sour cream. Blended low-fat cottage cheese and light sour cream provide for a lower-fat alternative that still has a creamy rich consistency. When using low-fat cheeses and milks in place of higher-fat creams you not only cut down on fat grams but add valuable calcium. This is significant when one considers that most women do not get their daily requirement of this important bone-strengthening mineral.

Per Serving: Calories 508; Total Fat 7 g; Saturated Fat 1 g; Cholesterol 93 mg; Sodium 715 mg; Carbohydrate 78 g; Fiber 9 g; Protein 36 g; Calcium 71 mg

Hearty Chicken and Borlotti Bean Stew

Wine: California Sauvignon Blanc   Makes 4 servings

1 cup dried borlotti beans (cranberry beans)
4 cups water
1 pound boneless skinless chicken breast halves, cut into 1/2-inch pieces
1 tablespoon olive oil
1 cup chopped tomato
1/4 cup chopped onion
1/4 cup chopped red bell pepper
1/4 cup chopped scallions
2 garlic cloves, minced
1 cup chicken stock
1 tablespoon chopped fresh basil
Salt and pepper to taste

Method of preparation

▼ Combine the borlotti beans and water in a saucepan. Bring to a boil; reduce heat.
▼ Simmer for 1 1/2 hours or until tender, stirring occasionally.
▼ Rinse the chicken and pat dry.
▼ Sauté the chicken in the olive oil in a saucepan over high heat until brown on both sides. Add the tomato, onion, red pepper, scallions and garlic and mix well.
▼ Cook, covered, for 10 minutes, stirring frequently. Add the stock and undrained beans and mix well.
▼ Simmer for 15 minutes or until of the desired consistency, stirring occasionally. Stir in the basil, salt and pepper.
▼ Serve immediately.

Borlotti beans, also known as cranberry beans or Roman beans, are buff-colored with reddish streaks. Nutritionally, legumes are low in fat and sodium and high in fiber, B-vitamins, and iron. The vitamin C-rich tomatoes will maximize the amount of iron you absorb from the legumes.

Per Serving: Calories 353; Total Fat 6 g; Saturated Fat 1 g; Cholesterol 66 mg; Sodium 127 mg; Carbohydrate 35 g; Fiber 14 g; Protein 39 g; Calcium 110 mg

Lemon Grass Curried Chicken

Wine: California Chardonnay   Makes 4 servings

1 1/2 pounds boneless skinless chicken breast halves, cut into 1/2-inch pieces
2 tablespoons olive oil
1 tablespoon curry paste
2 garlic cloves, minced
2 stalks lemon grass, chopped
2 tablespoons lime juice
1 tablespoon lime zest
1/2 cup chicken stock
1/2 teaspoon sugar
Salt and pepper to taste

Method of preparation
▼ Rinse the chicken and pat dry.
▼ Cook the olive oil and curry paste in a sauté pan over medium heat for 1 minute. Add the chicken and mix well.
▼ Sauté for 10 to 12 minutes. Stir in the garlic, lemon grass, lime juice and lime zest.
▼ Sauté for 2 minutes. Add the stock, sugar, salt and pepper and mix well.
▼ Simmer for 2 minutes, stirring frequently. Serve immediately.

Consuming chicken has become synonymous with healthy eating. When the skin and fat have been removed, chicken is low in fat as well as a good source of high-quality protein and a notable source for selenium and copper. Store chicken in the refrigerator, loosely wrapped in plastic wrap, for up to 2 days or freeze.

Per Serving: Calories 282; Total Fat 12 g; Saturated Fat 2 g; Cholesterol 99 mg; Sodium 229 mg; Carbohydrate 2 g; Fiber 1 g; Protein 40 g; Calcium 26 mg

Shredded Chicken with Snow Peas

Wine: Gentil   Makes 4 servings

1¹/2 pounds boneless skinless chicken breast halves
3 tablespoons minced shallots
3 garlic cloves, minced
¹/2 teaspoon red pepper flakes
1 tablespoon peanut oil
¹/2 cup chicken stock
2 stalks lemon grass, chopped
1 tablespoon lime juice
¹/2 cup julienned snow peas
¹/4 cup chopped scallions
Salt and black pepper to taste

Method of preparation
▼ Rinse the chicken and pat dry; shred.
▼ Sauté the shallots, garlic and red pepper flakes in the peanut oil in a nonstick skillet over medium heat for 3 minutes. Add the chicken and mix well.
▼ Sauté for 10 minutes. Stir in the stock, lemon grass and lime juice.
▼ Simmer for 4 to 5 minutes, stirring occasionally. Add the snow peas and scallions and mix well.
▼ Cook for 2 minutes, stirring frequently. Season with salt and black pepper.
▼ Spoon onto a heated serving platter. Serve immediately.

The type of oil used can enhance the quality of a dish. Peanut oil is often used in Japanese cooking and used here adds the taste and smell of "restaurant" quality cooking. The oil of peanuts is of the monounsaturated type, such as olive oil, and does not appear to have adverse effects on blood cholesterol. No matter what fat you use, try to keep the amount minimal.

Per Serving: Calories 244; Total Fat 6 g; Saturated Fat 1 g; Cholesterol 99 mg; Sodium 163 mg; Carbohydrate 4 g; Fiber 1 g; Protein 41 g; Calcium 40 mg

Smoked Breast of Chicken with Brandy Sauce

Wine: California Chardonnay   Makes 4 servings

1¹/₄ pounds boneless skinless chicken breast halves
4 ounces boneless skinless chicken breast halves, finely chopped
¹/₄ cup whipping cream
2 egg whites
1 tablespoon port wine
Salt and pepper to taste
1 cup dried fruit, finely chopped
1 cup chicken stock
1 tablespoon brandy

Method of preparation

▼ Rinse the chicken and pat dry. Pound 1¹/₄ pounds chicken breast halves ¹/₈ inch thick between sheets of plastic wrap with a meat mallet.
▼ Process the chopped chicken, whipping cream, egg whites, port wine, salt and pepper in a food processor until puréed. Combine the purée and dried fruit in a bowl and mix well.
▼ Spoon the purée mixture in the center of each chicken breast; roll to enclose the filling. Place seam side down in a smoker.
▼ Smoke for 35 minutes or until a meat thermometer registers 165 degrees.
▼ Combine the stock and brandy in a saucepan. Simmer for 3 minutes; keep warm.
▼ Cut the chicken rolls diagonally into 1-inch slices. Arrange on a heated serving platter; drizzle with the brandy sauce.

Yes, whipping cream! Weighing in at only eight grams of fat per serving, this recipe clearly illustrates that you can break the paradigm of having only low-fat foods in a low-fat entrée. Remember to use higher-fat ingredients sparingly and you just might be able to have your cake and eat it too.

Per Serving: Calories 333; Total Fat 8 g; Saturated Fat 4 g; Cholesterol 119 mg; Sodium 154 mg; Carbohydrate 18 g; Fiber 0 g; Protein 42 g; Calcium 41 mg

Breast of Turkey with Tomato Pepper Concassée

Wine: Chilean Sauvignon Blanc   Makes 4 servings

For the concassée

2 garlic cloves, minced
1 tablespoon olive oil
1 cup chopped tomato
1 cup chopped red bell pepper
1 jalapeño, chopped
Salt and pepper to taste

For the turkey

1 (1½-pound) boneless turkey breast
1 cup sliced mushrooms
½ cup sliced onion
10 savoy cabbage leaves
Salt and pepper to taste
¾ cup kasha
4 ounces ham, thinly sliced
2 teaspoons minced jalapeño
½ cup julienned red bell pepper
½ cup chopped fresh parsley

To prepare the concassée

▼ Sauté the garlic in the olive oil in a saucepan for 3 minutes. Add the tomato, red pepper, jalapeño, salt and pepper and mix well.
▼ Simmer, covered, for 20 to 30 minutes or until most of the liquid has evaporated.

To prepare the turkey

▼ Rinse and skin the turkey; pat dry. Butterfly the turkey to open like a book. Pound ¼ inch thick between sheets of plastic wrap with a meat mallet.
▼ Bring enough water to cover the mushrooms and onion to a boil in a saucepan. Add the mushrooms and onion.
▼ Blanch for 1 minute. Remove the mushrooms and onion with a slotted spoon to a bowl, reserving the liquid. Add the cabbage leaves to the reserved liquid.
▼ Blanch for 2 minutes. Drain and rinse with cold water.

To assemble

▼ Overlap the cabbage leaves into a 15x22-inch rectangle on a hard surface. Layer the turkey, salt, pepper, kasha, ham, mushroom mixture, jalapeño, red pepper and parsley in the order given over the cabbage. Roll into a cylinder shape to enclose the filling. Cover with plastic wrap; cover with foil and twist the ends.
▼ Bring a large saucepan filled with water to a boil; reduce heat. Add the cabbage roll.
▼ Simmer for 40 to 50 minutes or until the turkey registers an internal temperature of 165 degrees. Let stand for 10 minutes. Remove the foil. Cut through the plastic wrap into ¾-inch slices. Discard the plastic wrap.
▼ Arrange the slices on a heated serving platter. Top with the concassée.

Kasha is a delicious grain traditionally part of Eastern European diets. It is the kernel of the buckwheat seed (botanically a vegetable), also known as a "groat." Low in calories, kasha is a source of protein, iron, and B vitamins.

Per Serving: Calories 483; Total Fat 10 g; Saturated Fat 3 g; Cholesterol 118 mg; Sodium 633 mg; Carbohydrate 46 g; Fiber 9 g; Protein 55 g; Calcium 138 mg

Sautéed Turkey Mignons in Wine Sauce

Wine: French Chardonnay   Makes 4 servings

1 pound boneless skinless turkey breast, cut into 8 slices
Salt and pepper to taste
1 tablespoon butter
4 garlic cloves, minced
1 teaspoon thyme
$1/3$ cup sherry
$1/3$ cup chicken stock
2 tablespoons capers
2 tablespoons minced fresh parsley

Method of preparation

▼ Rinse the turkey and pat dry. Pound $1/4$ inch thick between sheets of plastic wrap with a meat mallet. Season with salt and pepper
▼ Sauté the turkey in the butter in a skillet over medium heat for 5 minutes per side or until light brown; do not overcook. Remove to a platter.
▼ Stir the garlic and thyme into the pan drippings in the skillet.
▼ Sauté for 2 minutes. Stir in the sherry.
▼ Cook over high heat until the sauce is reduced by $1/2$, stirring frequently. Add the stock and mix well.
▼ Cook over high heat until the sauce is reduced by $1/2$. Stir in the capers and parsley. Return the turkey to the skillet.
▼ Cook just until heated through, stirring frequently.
▼ Arrange the turkey on a heated serving platter; drizzle with the sauce.

Capers are pickled pellet-shaped buds that add a zesty tang to any dish. Virtually void of any calories, they contain a minimal amount of salt. Look for capers in your supermarket, where they'll most likely be located near the pickles and olives.

Per Serving: Calories 191; Total Fat 5 g; Saturated Fat 2 g; Cholesterol 76 mg; Sodium 150 mg; Carbohydrate 3 g; Fiber 0 g; Protein 27 g; Calcium 56 mg

Tandoori-Style Turkey

Wine: California Sauvignon Blanc   Makes 4 servings

4 (4-ounce) turkey cutlets
1/2 cup plain nonfat yogurt
1 1/2 tablespoons grated gingerroot
1 tablespoon lemon juice
2 teaspoons paprika
1/2 teaspoon salt
1/2 teaspoon cinnamon
1/2 teaspoon cumin
1/8 teaspoon pepper
2 garlic cloves, minced

Method of preparation
▼ Rinse the turkey and pat dry. Pound between sheets of plastic wrap with a meat mallet until flattened. Arrange in a dish.
▼ Combine the yogurt, gingerroot, lemon juice, paprika, salt, cinnamon, cumin, pepper and garlic in a bowl and mix well. Pour over the turkey, turning to coat.
▼ Marinate in the refrigerator for 8 to 10 hours, turning occasionally. Drain, reserving the marinade.
▼ Preheat the grill. Spray the grill rack with nonstick cooking spray.
▼ Grill over medium-hot coals for 6 to 7 minutes per side or until cooked through, basting frequently with the reserved marinade.
▼ Arrange the turkey on a heated serving platter. Serve immediately.

Yogurt is used extensively in Middle Eastern and Indian dishes. Versatile in cooking, yogurt is packed with calcium and is a good source of protein. Many individuals cannot digest lactose-containing dairy products because they do not have enough of the enzyme necessary to break it down. No problem with yogurt since it contains bacterial cultures that virtually do the digesting for them.

Per Serving: Calories 156; Total Fat 2 g; Saturated Fat 1 g; Cholesterol 69 mg; Sodium 361 mg; Carbohydrate 4 g; Fiber 1 g; Protein 29 g; Calcium 82 mg

The Most Incredible Meat Loaf Ever!

Wine: Chianti   Makes 4 servings

For the vegetable filling
1 cup finely chopped red bell pepper
1 cup finely chopped tomato
1 small zucchini, finely chopped
1/2 cup chopped scallions
2 teaspoons chopped fresh basil
Salt and pepper to taste

For the meat loaf
1/2 cup soft bread crumbs
1/2 cup skim milk
1/4 cup minced Italian parsley
2 egg whites
2 garlic cloves, minced
1/2 teaspoon oregano
1 pound ground turkey
Salt and pepper to taste
1/2 cup shredded part skim milk
    mozzarella cheese

To prepare the vegetable filling
▼ Steam the red pepper, tomato, zucchini, scallions and basil in a steamer until tender. Season with salt and pepper.

To prepare the meat loaf
▼ Preheat the oven to 350 degrees.
▼ Combine the bread crumbs, skim milk, parsley, egg whites, garlic and oregano in a bowl, stirring until of a paste consistency. Add the ground turkey, salt and pepper and mix well.
▼ Place the ground turkey mixture between 2 sheets of heavy-duty plastic wrap. Roll with a rolling pin into a 1/4-inch thick rectangle; discard the top sheet of plastic wrap. Spread the vegetable mixture over the rectangle; sprinkle with the cheese. Roll into a cylinder shape on the plastic wrap to enclose the filling; wrap with plastic wrap. Wrap with foil and twist the ends. Place on a baking sheet.
▼ Bake for 1 hour or until a meat thermometer registers 165 degrees.

To assemble
▼ Unwrap; cut at a 45-degree angle into 3/4-inch slices.
▼ Arrange on a heated serving platter. Serve immediately.

     Another paradigm breaker, since this loaf is really a roll and poultry is used in place of beef. Extra-lean beef or a combination of beef and turkey can be used although you will add fat grams. This loaf is so moist you will not need a sauce, but if you prefer one, serve with a light marinara sauce.

Per Serving: Calories 358; Total Fat 14 g; Saturated Fat 5 g; Cholesterol 98 mg; Sodium 412 mg; Carbohydrate 27 g; Fiber 3 g; Protein 31 g; Calcium 206 mg

Roasted Catfish with Caramelized Onions

Wine: Sauvignon Blanc   Makes 4 servings

2 cups julienned red onions
1 tablespoon olive oil
4 strips orange zest
1/4 cup thinly sliced black olives
1 teaspoon minced fresh oregano
1 1/2 pounds catfish fillets
1/4 cup orange juice
Salt and pepper to taste

Method of preparation
▼ Preheat the oven to 400 degrees.
▼ Combine the red onions, olive oil and orange zest in a bowl and mix well. Spoon into a baking dish.
▼ Bake for 25 minutes or just until the onions begin to brown. Stir in the olives and oregano.
▼ Arrange the catfish in a single layer in a baking dish. Add the orange juice, salt, pepper and onion mixture.
▼ Bake for 15 to 18 minutes or until the fish flakes easily. Serve immediately.

Catfish is most often found in the southern and central parts of the United States, although government-regulated farming has made it more widely available. Farmed catfish has firm, moist, white flesh and a delicate flavor. Freshwater catfish tops the list of rich sources of magnesium, a mineral involved in bone metabolism.

Per Serving: Calories 108; Total Fat 5 g; Saturated Fat 1 g; Cholesterol 18 mg; Sodium 90 mg; Carbohydrate 11 g; Fiber 2 g; Protein 6 g; Calcium 43 mg

Spicy Cajun Catfish

Wine: California Chardonnay   Makes 4 servings

1¹/₄ pounds catfish fillets
2 teaspoons olive oil
¹/₄ cup dry bread crumbs
1¹/₂ teaspoons paprika
¹/₂ teaspoon garlic powder
¹/₂ teaspoon black pepper
¹/₂ teaspoon cayenne
¹/₂ teaspoon salt
¹/₂ teaspoon cumin
2 tablespoons lime juice
1 tablespoon butter

Method of preparation
▼ Brush both sides of the catfish with the olive oil. Pat a mixture of the bread crumbs, paprika, garlic powder, black pepper, cayenne, salt and cumin on each side of the fillets.
▼ Spray a nonstick skillet with nonstick cooking spray. Brown the catfish in the prepared skillet over medium heat for 2 to 3 minutes per side or until the fish flakes easily. Remove the fish to a warm platter.
▼ Add the lime juice to the skillet. Cook until slightly reduced. Remove from heat. Add the butter, stirring until blended. Drizzle over the catfish. Serve immediately.

The secret is in the spices. Cajun-style foods rely on the cook's creativity. Use your personal concoction on your favorite fish, as well as meats. Spicy and sensational, this dish is nicely complemented by New Orleans red beans and rice.

Per Serving: Calories 195; Total Fat 9 g; Saturated Fat 3 g; Cholesterol 90 mg; Sodium 371 mg; Carbohydrate 3 g; Fiber 1 g; Protein 24 g; Calcium 29 mg

Broiled Grouper Over Chiffonade of Braised Savoy

Wine: Pouilly-Fuissé   Makes 4 servings

1 1/2 pounds grouper fillets
1 tablespoon melted butter
2 tablespoons lemon juice
1/2 teaspoon cumin
1/2 cup julienned red onion
2 garlic cloves, julienned
1 tablespoon olive oil
3 cups shredded savoy cabbage
1/2 cup chopped red tomato
1/4 teaspoon caraway seeds, crushed
Salt and pepper to taste

Method of preparation

▼ Place the grouper in a dish. Brush both sides of the fillets with the butter; drizzle with the lemon juice. Sprinkle with the cumin.
▼ Sauté the red onion and garlic in the olive oil in a saucepan over medium heat for 1 minute; reduce heat. Add the cabbage and mix well.
▼ Simmer, covered, for 5 to 6 minutes, stirring occasionally. Stir in the tomato, caraway seeds, salt and pepper. Cook just until heated through, stirring frequently.
▼ Preheat the broiler.
▼ Arrange the fish on a broiler rack. Broil 4 to 5 inches from the heat source for 4 to 5 minutes per side or until the fish flakes easily.
▼ Spoon the chiffonade onto a warm platter; top with the grouper. Serve immediately.

Red grouper, found primarily off the Florida and Gulf coasts, is the most common grouper in the United States. Although more expensive, and not as mild and sweet tasting, a black variety is also available. Peak season for this fish is between January and April. It makes a nice substitute for the more expensive red snapper.

Per Serving: Calories 244; Total Fat 8 g; Saturated Fat 3 g; Cholesterol 71 mg; Sodium 137 mg; Carbohydrate 7 g; Fiber 2 g; Protein 35 g; Calcium 77 mg

Broiled Halibut in Horseradish Ginger Crust

Wine: Lakespring Chardonnay   Makes 4 servings

For the sauce

2 tablespoons soy sauce
2 tablespoons sherry
1 tablespoon rice vinegar
1 tablespoon water

For the halibut

1 1/2 pounds halibut steaks, 1/2-inch thick
Salt and pepper to taste
1 1/2 cups bread crumbs
2 tablespoons minced scallions
1 tablespoon olive oil
1 tablespoon grated gingerroot
1 tablespoon sherry
1 1/2 teaspoons grated horseradish

To prepare the sauce

▼ Combine the soy sauce, sherry, rice vinegar and water in a bowl and mix well.

To prepare the halibut

▼ Preheat the broiler.
▼ Spray both sides of the halibut with nonstick cooking spray. Season with salt and pepper. Arrange on a broiler rack.
▼ Broil for 4 to 5 minutes per side.
▼ Combine the bread crumbs, scallions, olive oil, gingerroot, sherry and horseradish in a bowl and mix well. Sprinkle over the halibut.
▼ Broil 5 inches from the heat source until the fish is brown and flakes easily; do not overcook.

To assemble

▼ Place the halibut on a warm platter; drizzle with the sauce.
▼ Serve immediately.

Halibut is a firm flat fish belonging to the flounder family. It is found in the North Atlantic and North Pacific oceans. Considered by some as the most desirable of the white-flesh fishes, halibut is an excellent source of low-fat, low-calorie protein. When purchasing, select fresh fish that does not have a "fishy" odor.

Per Serving: Calories 401; Total Fat 10 g; Saturated Fat 2 g; Cholesterol 54 mg; Sodium 792 mg; Carbohydrate 32 g; Fiber 1 g; Protein 41 g; Calcium 117 mg

Curry-Spiced Halibut Steak

Wine: Chilean Chardonnay   Makes 4 servings

For the halibut

1 teaspoon curry powder
1/4 teaspoon salt
1/4 teaspoon cumin
1/8 teaspoon turmeric
1/8 teaspoon cayenne
1 garlic clove, minced
1 1/2 pounds halibut steaks, 3/4-inch thick

For the sauce

1/4 cup plain nonfat yogurt
1 tablespoon chopped fresh cilantro
Salt and pepper to taste

To prepare the halibut

▼ Combine the curry powder, salt, cumin, turmeric, cayenne and garlic in a bowl and mix well. Rub both sides of the halibut with the spice mixture. Place in a dish.
▼ Chill for 1 hour.
▼ Preheat the oven to 375 degrees.
▼ Place the halibut in a single layer in a baking dish sprayed with nonstick cooking spray; do not crowd.
▼ Bake for 18 to 20 minutes or until the fish flakes easily.

To prepare the sauce

▼ Spoon the pan drippings into a bowl. Add the yogurt, cilantro, salt and pepper, whisking until mixed.

To assemble

▼ Arrange the halibut on a warm platter. Drizzle with the sauce.

Thoughtful presentation with seafood is essential. A colorful, attractive arrangement of seafood, especially of white-fleshed fish, will enhance your enjoyment of the meal. Add color with parsley, lemons, carrots, tomatoes, or black olives, which contrast nicely with fish and complement its flavor.

Per Serving: Calories 200; Total Fat 4 g; Saturated Fat 1 g; Cholesterol 55 mg; Sodium 238 mg; Carbohydrate 2 g; Fiber 0 g; Protein 36 g; Calcium 119 mg

Grilled Barbequed Halibut Steak

Wine: Pouilly-Fuissé   Makes 4 servings

For the sauce

1/2 cup honey
1/4 cup rice vinegar
1/4 cup ketchup
2 tablespoons tamari
1 teaspoon chopped gingerroot
1/2 teaspoon cardamom
1/2 teaspoon coriander
1/4 teaspoon cloves
2 star anise
2 garlic cloves, crushed

For the halibut

1 1/2 pounds halibut steaks
2 tablespoons olive oil
1 teaspoon fennel seeds, roasted

To prepare the sauce

▼ Combine the honey, rice vinegar, ketchup, tamari, gingerroot, cardamom, coriander, cloves, star anise and garlic in a saucepan and mix well. Bring to a boil; reduce heat.
▼ Simmer for 20 minutes, stirring occasionally.

To prepare the halibut

▼ Preheat the grill.
▼ Brush both sides of the halibut with the olive oil; sprinkle both sides with the fennel seeds.
▼ Grill the halibut over medium-hot coals for 2 to 3 minutes per side. Brush each side of the halibut with the sauce.
▼ Grill for 4 to 5 minutes per side longer or until the fish flakes easily, basting with the sauce at 1-minute intervals.

To assemble

▼ Arrange the halibut on a warm serving platter. Serve immediately.

Fennel seeds are a fantastic flavoring for fish. To roast fennel seeds, place one teaspoon fennel seeds in a small skillet. Cook over medium heat for 5 to 6 minutes, shaking the skillet constantly. Cool the fennel seeds and crush with your fingertips.

Per Serving: Calories 415; Total Fat 11 g; Saturated Fat 2 g; Cholesterol 54 mg; Sodium 678 mg; Carbohydrate 43 g; Fiber 1 g; Protein 37 g; Calcium 120 mg

Roasted Monkfish with White Bean Compote

Wine: French Rully   Makes 4 servings

For the compote

1/4 cup chopped scallions
1/4 cup chopped red bell pepper
1/4 cup chopped red tomato
1 tablespoon olive oil
1 tablespoon chopped fresh basil
1 (16-ounce) can white beans, drained, rinsed
Salt and pepper to taste

For the monkfish

1 1/2 pounds monkfish
4 garlic cloves, slivered
Salt and pepper to taste
1 tablespoon butter
1/2 cup white wine

To prepare the compote

▼ Combine the scallions, red pepper, tomato, olive oil and basil in a saucepan and mix well. Bring to a boil; reduce heat.
▼ Simmer for 5 minutes, stirring occasionally. Stir in the white beans.
▼ Simmer for 5 minutes, stirring occasionally. Season with salt and pepper.

To prepare the monkfish

▼ Preheat the oven to 350 degrees.
▼ Remove the skin from each monkfish tail. Rinse and pat dry.
▼ Make several slits in each tail with a small knife. Insert a sliver of garlic into each slit. Season with salt and pepper.
▼ Sauté the monkfish in the butter in an ovenproof dish until brown on both sides. Pour the wine over the fish.
▼ Bake for 15 minutes.

To assemble

▼ Cut the monkfish diagonally into 1/4-inch slices.
▼ Spoon the compote onto a warm platter. Top with the sliced monkfish. Serve immediately.

Perhaps since monkfish is also known as lawyerfish and its head is exceptionally ugly, cooks may veer away from preparing this sea creature. The only edible portion of this fish is the tail. The flesh is sweet, dense, boneless, and similar in taste to lobster. Like most fish, it is a good source of high-quality protein, while low in fat, cholesterol, and sodium.

Per Serving: Calories 373; Total Fat 9 g; Saturated Fat 3 g; Cholesterol 50 mg; Sodium 71 mg; Carbohydrate 31 g; Fiber 8 g; Protein 36 g; Calcium 131 mg

Baked Salmon with Hoisin Mustard Glaze

Wine: Riesling   Makes 4 servings

2 tablespoons hoisin sauce
2 tablespoons tamari
2 tablespoons orange juice
1 tablespoon Dijon mustard
2 garlic cloves, crushed
4 (6-ounce) salmon fillets

Method of preparation

▼ Combine the hoisin sauce, tamari, orange juice, Dijon mustard and garlic in a saucepan and mix well.
▼ Cook over medium heat until of the consistency of a glaze and heated through, stirring constantly. Cool to room temperature.
▼ Pour the glaze over the salmon in a dish, turning to coat.
▼ Chill in the refrigerator for 15 minutes. Drain, reserving the glaze. Place the salmon in a baking dish sprayed with nonstick cooking spray.
▼ Preheat the oven to 350 degrees.
▼ Bake for 25 minutes or until the fish flakes easily, basting with the reserved glaze frequently.
▼ Arrange the salmon on a warm platter. Serve immediately.

A calorie counter's dream, this recipe is low in calories and fat. Other varieties of fish, such as flounder, can be substituted for the salmon, adjusting the cooking times to the thickness of the fillet.

Per Serving: Calories 104; Total Fat 4 g; Saturated Fat 1 g; Cholesterol 34 mg; Sodium 495 mg; Carbohydrate 4 g; Fiber 0 g; Protein 14 g; Calcium 17 mg

Chilled Salmon with Cucumbers and Fresh Herb Sauce

Wine: French Chablis   Makes 4 servings

For the salmon

3/4 cup white wine
2 cups vegetable broth
1/2 cup sliced onion
1/4 cup chopped celery
1/2 teaspoon thyme
1/2 teaspoon basil
1/2 teaspoon peppercorns
2 bay leaves
1 1/2 pounds salmon steaks

For the sauce

1/4 cup nonfat mayonnaise
1/4 cup nonfat sour cream
2 tablespoons chopped scallions
1 tablespoon lemon juice
1 tablespoon chopped fresh dillweed
1/8 teaspoon saffron
1 cup thinly sliced English cucumber

For the salmon

▼ Combine the white wine, broth, onion, celery, thyme, basil, peppercorns and bay leaves in a poacher and mix well. Bring to a boil.
▼ Simmer for 30 minutes. Place the salmon in the poaching liquid.
▼ Poach for 15 minutes. Remove the salmon to a platter.
▼ Chill, covered, in the refrigerator.

For the sauce

▼ Combine the mayonnaise, sour cream, scallions, lemon juice, dillweed and saffron in a bowl and mix well.

To assemble

▼ Debone the salmon carefully, leaving the fish intact. Place on a serving platter.
▼ Spread the sauce over the top of the salmon. Arrange the cucumber slices decoratively over the salmon. Serve immediately.

Saffron has been known to fetch a price of $2,000 per pound, putting the price tag of a pinch at several dollars. Real saffron is from Spain and consists of the dried stamens of the saffron crocus. An acceptable substitution is turmeric. Use twice as much as the amount of saffron called for and it will add the characteristic yellow color, but not necessarily the flavor.

Per Serving: Calories 274; Total Fat 6 g; Saturated Fat 1 g; Cholesterol 91 mg; Sodium 403 mg; Carbohydrate 10 g; Fiber 1 g; Protein 36 g; Calcium 75 mg

Roasted Salmon with Sautéed Spinach

Wine: French Chardonnay   Makes 4 servings

1 cup dry bread crumbs
1 tablespoon minced fresh basil
3 teaspoons olive oil
1 teaspoon grated lemon zest
1 garlic clove, minced
Salt and pepper to taste
1 (1¹/₂ pound) salmon fillet, cut into 6-ounce pieces
1 pound fresh spinach, trimmed
2 leeks, julienned
1 teaspoon olive oil

Method of preparation
▼ Preheat the oven to 350 degrees.
▼ Combine the bread crumbs, basil, 3 teaspoons olive oil, lemon zest, garlic, salt and pepper in a bowl and mix well.
▼ Coat the salmon with the bread crumb mixture. Arrange skin side down on a baking sheet.
▼ Bake for 15 minutes or until the fish flakes easily.
▼ Sauté the spinach and leeks in 1 teaspoon olive oil in a skillet just until wilted. Season with salt and pepper.
▼ Spoon equal amounts of the spinach mixture onto 4 heated plates. Top with the salmon. Serve immediately.

Aquaculture has greatly increased the availability of mild-flavored salmon. Although one of the more fatty varieties of fish, salmon is rich in Omega-3 fatty acids. The Omega-3-rich diet of Eskimos appears to be responsible for reduced blood clotting; blood clots are one of the major causes of heart attacks. Other varieties of Omega-3-rich fish include mackerel, herring, Atlantic halibut, and sardines.

Per Serving: Calories 303; Total Fat 11 g; Saturated Fat 2 g; Cholesterol 89 mg; Sodium 257 mg; Carbohydrate 12 g; Fiber 5 g; Protein 39 g; Calcium 173 mg

Grilled Red Snapper Mediterranean

Wine: French Sancerre   Makes 4 servings

For the sauce

1/2 cup chopped red tomato
1/4 cup red wine
1 tablespoon olive oil
2 teaspoons green peppercorns
2 teaspoons capers
1/4 teaspoon thyme
1/4 teaspoon rosemary
1/4 teaspoon basil
Salt and pepper to taste

For the red snapper

1/4 cup julienned carrot
1/4 cup julienned fennel
1/4 cup julienned snow peas
11/2 pounds red snapper fillets
Salt and pepper to taste
1 tablespoon olive oil

To prepare the sauce
▼ Combine the tomato, red wine, olive oil, peppercorns and capers in a saucepan and mix well. Bring to a boil; reduce heat.
▼ Simmer for 5 minutes, stirring occasionally. Stir in the thyme, rosemary, basil, salt and pepper.

To prepare the red snapper
▼ Preheat the grill.
▼ Combine the carrot and fennel with enough water to cover in a saucepan. Bring to a boil; reduce heat.
▼ Simmer until the vegetables are tender. Remove the vegetables with a slotted spoon to a platter, reserving the liquid. Add the snow peas to the reserved liquid.
▼ Cook for 2 minutes. Remove with a slotted spoon to a platter.
▼ Season the red snapper with salt and pepper. Brush with the olive oil. Place the fish in a fish rack.
▼ Grill over hot coals for 2 to 3 minutes per side or until the fish flakes easily.

To assemble
▼ Arrange the fillets on a heated serving platter.
▼ Top each fillet with some of the vegetable mixture; drizzle with the sauce. Serve immediately.

A tropical water fish, red snapper is a white, sweet meat. Fresh fish should be prepared immediately. If this is not possible, wrap the fish in moisture-proof wrapping, store in the refrigerator, and prepare within one day.

Per Serving: Calories 256; Total Fat 9 g; Saturated Fat 1 g; Cholesterol 63 mg; Sodium 152 mg; Carbohydrate 3 g; Fiber 1 g; Protein 36 g; Calcium 71 mg

Roasted Red Snapper with Tomatoes and Leeks

Wine: Meursault   Makes 4 servings

For the sauce
3 garlic cloves, minced
1 tablespoon olive oil
1 cup sliced leek bulbs
2 cups chopped tomatoes
1 cup white wine
1/2 cup chopped fresh parsley
2 tablespoons chopped fresh dillweed
Salt and pepper to taste

For the red snapper
1 1/2 pounds red snapper fillets
1 tablespoon cumin, crushed
1 1/2 teaspoons pepper

To prepare the sauce
▼ Sauté the garlic in the olive oil in a saucepan for 2 to 3 minutes. Add the leeks.
▼ Sauté for 2 minutes longer. Stir in the tomatoes and white wine. Bring to a boil; reduce heat.
▼ Simmer for 5 minutes, stirring occasionally. Add the parsley, dillweed, salt and pepper and mix well.

To prepare the red snapper
▼ Preheat the oven to 350 degrees.
▼ Sprinkle both sides of the red snapper with the cumin and pepper. Arrange skin side down in a baking dish sprayed with nonstick cooking spray. Spoon the sauce over the fish.
▼ Bake for 25 minutes or until the fish flakes easily.

To assemble
▼ Arrange the red snapper on a heated serving platter.
▼ Spoon the pan drippings over the fish. Serve immediately.

Dillweed is an herb that was once thought to ward off witches and cure hiccups, and perhaps this is the reason it has become so widely used. Easily grown on a windowsill, dillweed is an annual plant that likes full sun and well-drained soil. When planted outdoors, the plants will usually reseed themselves in the fall.

Per Serving: Calories 308; Total Fat 7 g; Saturated Fat 1 g; Cholesterol 63 mg; Sodium 136 mg; Carbohydrate 15 g; Fiber 2 g; Protein 38 g; Calcium 155 mg

Grilled Swordfish with Citrus Salsa

Wine: California Chardonnay   Makes 4 servings

For the salsa
Sections of 1 ruby red grapefruit
Sections of 1 orange
Sections of 1 lime
1/2 cup chopped red bell pepper
1/4 cup chopped red onion
1 tablespoon chopped fresh basil
1 ounce tequila
Salt and pepper to taste

For the swordfish
1 1/2 pounds swordfish steaks
1 tablespoon olive oil

To prepare the salsa
▼ Combine the grapefruit, orange, lime, red pepper, red onion, basil, tequila, salt and pepper in a bowl and mix well.
▼ Chill, covered, in the refrigerator.

To prepare the swordfish
▼ Preheat the grill.
▼ Sauté the swordfish on both sides in the olive oil in a nonstick skillet until light brown.
▼ Place the swordfish on the grill rack 4 inches above hot coals.
▼ Grill for 5 to 6 minutes per side or until the fish flakes easily.

To assemble
▼ Arrange the swordfish on a heated platter. Top with the salsa.
▼ Serve immediately.

Who says salsa has to be spicy and have tomatoes? This salsa, or sauce, gets its kick from several citrus items that also add significant amounts of vitamin C. The tequila may be omitted, but it does add a nice flavor.

Per Serving: Calories 320; Total Fat 10 g; Saturated Fat 2 g; Cholesterol 66 mg; Sodium 154 mg; Carbohydrate 17 g; Fiber 3 g; Protein 35 g; Calcium 45 mg

Oven-Roasted Tuna Steaks Teriyaki

Wine: French Chablis   Makes 4 servings

1/2 cup pineapple juice
2 tablespoons soy sauce
2 tablespoons sake
1 tablespoon minced gingerroot
1 tablespoon sesame oil
1 1/2 pounds tuna steaks

Method of preparation

▼ Combine the pineapple juice, soy sauce, sake, gingerroot and sesame oil in a bowl and mix well. Pour over the tuna in a dish, turning to coat.
▼ Marinate, covered, in the refrigerator for 3 hours, turning occasionally.
▼ Preheat the oven to 400 degrees.
▼ Drain the tuna, reserving the marinade. Place the tuna on a baking sheet.
▼ Bake for 6 minutes per side or until the tuna flakes easily, basting occasionally with the reserved marinade.
▼ Arrange the tuna on a heated serving platter. Serve immediately.

Canned tuna is often the only type of tuna many individuals have ever experienced. Give fresh tuna a whirl . . . it's great! Similar to swordfish in texture and flavor, fresh tuna is readily available from April to September. Frozen varieties work well, and are available all year long. Tuna contains all the essential amino acids, making it a top-quality protein.

Per Serving: Calories 307; Total Fat 12 g; Saturated Fat 3 g; Cholesterol 65 mg; Sodium 481 mg; Carbohydrate 5 g; Fiber 0 g; Protein 40 g; Calcium 20 mg

Roasted Corn and Crab Cakes

Wine: Chilean Chardonnay   Makes 4 servings

1 pound crab meat, flaked
1 cup fresh bread crumbs
3/4 cup light mayonnaise
1/2 cup chopped red bell pepper
2 ears corn on the cob, roasted, scraped
1 bunch scallions, chopped
1 egg, beaten
3 tablespoons Worcestershire sauce
1 tablespoon garlic paste
1 teaspoon Old Bay seasoning
1 teaspoon Tabasco sauce
1/2 cup dry bread crumbs
1 tablespoon vegetable oil

Method of preparation

▼ Combine the crab meat, fresh bread crumbs, mayonnaise, red pepper, corn, scallions, egg, Worcestershire sauce, garlic paste, Old Bay seasoning and Tabasco sauce in a bowl and mix well.
▼ Portion 2-ounce balls with an ice cream scoop; flatten slightly. Coat with the dry bread crumbs.
▼ Sauté the cakes in the vegetable oil in a nonstick skillet until brown on both sides. Remove to a 200-degree oven to keep warm until serving time.

Commercially packaged crab meat is usually of the blue crab variety and is available in several grades. Lump crab meat, consisting of large pieces with no fragments of shell, is the best type. Like most shellfish, crab is very low in fat and modest in calories.

Per Serving: Calories 295; Total Fat 11 g; Saturated Fat 3 g; Cholesterol 161 mg; Sodium 767 mg; Carbohydrate 27 g; Fiber 3 g; Protein 26 g; Calcium 165 mg

Grilled Chili-Dusted Sea Scallops on Black Bean Compote

Wine: California Sauvignon Blanc   Makes 4 servings

For the compote

2 cups cooked black beans
1/4 cup (1/4-inch pieces) red onion
1/4 cup (1/4-inch pieces) celery
1/4 cup (1/4-inch pieces) red tomato
3 tablespoons lime juice
2 tablespoons chopped fresh basil
1 tablespoon sesame oil
1/2 teaspoon cumin
1 jalapeño, chopped
Salt and pepper to taste

For the scallops

1 pound sea scallops
1 tablespoon olive oil
Salt and pepper to taste
3 tablespoons chili powder
1 teaspoon cumin

To prepare the compote
▼ Combine the black beans, red onion, celery, tomato, lime juice, basil, sesame oil, cumin, jalapeño, salt and pepper in a bowl and mix well.

To prepare the scallops
▼ Preheat the grill.
▼ Combine the scallops, olive oil, salt and pepper in a bowl and mix gently.
▼ Coat the scallops with a mixture of the chili powder and cumin.
▼ Grill over medium-hot coals for 6 to 7 minutes, turning frequently to prevent burning.

To assemble
▼ Spoon the compote onto a chilled platter. Arrange the scallops over the compote.
▼ Serve immediately.

Basil can truly be considered "king" of the herbs, considering its Greek derivation means kingly and its addition to any recipe makes it a regal affair. A fairly good source of potassium, sweet basil is a common garden variety growing to about eighteen inches in height. The leaves will darken quickly after cutting, so use the herb immediately. Basil is a superb complement to tomatoes. Flavors are most outstanding when served at room temperature.

Per Serving: Calories 314; Total Fat 9 g; Saturated Fat 1 g; Cholesterol 37 mg; Sodium 251 mg; Carbohydrate 32 g; Fiber 11 g; Protein 28 g; Calcium 129 mg

Citrus Shrimp with Mango Sauce

Wine: Riesling   Makes 4 servings

Zest of 2 lemons
1 tablespoon minced poblano pepper
Juice of 2 lemons
3 tablespoons brown sugar
12 large shrimp, peeled, deveined, butterflied
1 tablespoon olive oil
1 cup sliced mango
1 tablespoon grated gingerroot
1 ounce dark rum

Method of preparation

▼ Combine the lemon zest and poblano pepper in a bowl and mix well.
▼ Combine the lemon juice and brown sugar in a saucepan. Bring to a simmer, stirring occasionally. Add the lemon zest mixture and mix well. Coat both sides of the shrimp with the mixture.
▼ Heat the olive oil in a skillet until hot. Add the shrimp.
▼ Sauté for 1 minute per side. Stir in the mango and gingerroot.
▼ Cook for 1 minute, stirring constantly. Add the rum and mix well.
▼ Cook for 1 minute, stirring constantly.
▼ Arrange the shrimp on a heated platter; drizzle with the sauce. Serve immediately.

Slippery, succulent, and sweet are words that describe the luscious ripe mango. Mangoes are ripe when the fruit yields to gentle pressure and exhibits a sweet fragrance. Underripe fruit may be placed in a paper bag and allowed to stand at room temperature for several days to ripen. Like most yellow-orange fruits and vegetables, mangoes are a great source of vitamin A.

Per Serving: Calories 153; Total Fat 4 g; Saturated Fat 1 g; Cholesterol 59 mg; Sodium 63 mg; Carbohydrate 20 g; Fiber 1 g; Protein 9 g; Calcium 64 mg

Down-East Shrimp Étouffée

Wine: California Sauvignon Blanc   Makes 4 servings

1 cup chopped onion
$1/2$ cup chopped celery
2 tablespoons olive oil
$1/2$ cup chopped green bell pepper
2 garlic cloves, minced
$1/2$ teaspoon white pepper
$1/2$ teaspoon paprika
$1/4$ teaspoon cayenne
1 tablespoon flour
1 cup chicken stock
$1/2$ cup chopped tomato
1 pound shrimp, peeled, deveined
1 cup chopped scallions
2 cups hot cooked rice
$1/4$ cup chopped fresh parsley

Method of preparation
▼ Sauté the onion and celery in the olive oil in a saucepan for 5 to 6 minutes. Stir in the green pepper and garlic.
▼ Sauté for 3 to 4 minutes. Add the white pepper, paprika and cayenne and mix well.
▼ Sauté for 2 minutes. Stir in the flour. Add the stock and tomato and mix well. Bring to a simmer.
▼ Simmer for 3 to 4 minutes, stirring frequently. Add the shrimp and scallions and mix well.
▼ Simmer for 6 to 7 minutes or until the shrimp turn pink, stirring occasionally.
▼ Spoon the rice onto a heated platter. Top with the shrimp étouffée and sprinkle with the parsley.
▼ Serve immediately.

Shrimp is high in cholesterol when compared to other seafood. Don't despair—saturated fat and total fat are more the culprits in raising the blood cholesterol value on your laboratory analysis than the actual cholesterol content of a food. Since shrimp is low in fat and saturated fat, it fits into a heart-healthy diet.

Per Serving: Calories 353; Total Fat 9 g; Saturated Fat 1 g; Cholesterol 173 mg; Sodium 341 mg; Carbohydrate 38 g; Fiber 3 g; Protein 28 g; Calcium 125 mg

Pan-Seared Indian Shrimp with Arugula Tabouli

Wine: Riesling   Makes 4 servings

For the tabouli
4 ounces bulgur
1/4 cup lime juice
1 red bell pepper, chopped into 1/8-inch
   pieces
2 large tomatoes, peeled, seeded,
   chopped
1 cucumber, peeled, seeded, chopped
3 scallions, finely chopped
1 cup finely chopped arugula
1/4 teaspoon cayenne
Salt and black pepper to taste

For the shrimp
1 cup plain nonfat yogurt
1/4 cup lemon juice
1 tablespoon cumin
1 teaspoon turmeric
1/2 teaspoon fennel seeds, crushed
Paprika to taste
12 large shrimp, peeled, deveined
2 tablespoons olive oil

To prepare the tabouli
▼ Combine the bulgur with enough warm water to cover in a bowl and mix well. Let
   stand for 1 hour; drain.
▼ Combine the lime juice, red pepper, tomatoes, cucumber, scallions, arugula and
   cayenne in a bowl and mix well. Stir in the bulgur. Season with salt and black pepper.

To prepare the shrimp
▼ Combine the yogurt, lemon juice, cumin, turmeric, fennel seeds and paprika in a
   bowl and mix well. Combine the shrimp with 1/2 of the yogurt mixture in a bowl and
   mix well, reserving the remaining yogurt mixture.
▼ Remove the shrimp, discarding the yogurt mixture. Sauté the shrimp in the olive oil in
   a skillet for 2 minutes per side or until the shrimp turn pink.

To assemble
▼ Spoon 1/4 cup tabouli in the center of each of 4 chilled salad plates.
▼ Arrange 3 shrimp around the tabouli on each salad plate. Drizzle 1 tablespoon of the
   reserved yogurt mixture over the shrimp.
▼ Serve immediately.

Bulgur, or cracked wheat, is sometimes referred to as the "rice of the Middle
East." Usually found in health food stores, yet sometimes found in supermarkets,
this nutty-flavored grain is available in three grinds: fine, medium, and coarse.
Tabouli utilizes the finest of the grinds.

Per Serving: Calories 280; Total Fat 9 g; Saturated Fat 1 g; Cholesterol 60 mg; Sodium 120 mg;
Carbohydrate 37 g; Fiber 4 g; Protein 17 g; Calcium 195 mg
Nutritional profile includes the entire amount of the yogurt sauce.

Shrimp and Crab Gumbo Creole

Wine: Sauvignon Blanc   Makes 4 servings

1 cup chopped onion
1/2 cup chopped celery
3 garlic cloves, minced
1 tablespoon olive oil
1/2 cup chopped green bell pepper
1/2 cup chopped red bell pepper
1/4 teaspoon cayenne
Salt and black pepper to taste
3 cups chicken stock
2 cups chopped red tomatoes
1 1/2 pounds okra, cut into 1/2-inch slices
1 pound shrimp, peeled, deveined
8 ounces crab meat, flaked
1 tablespoon filé powder
2 cups hot cooked rice

Method of preparation
▼ Sauté the onion, celery and garlic in the olive oil in a stockpot over medium heat for 5 to 7 minutes. Add the bell peppers, cayenne, salt and black pepper and mix well.
▼ Sauté for 5 minutes. Stir in the stock and tomatoes. Bring to a boil; reduce heat.
▼ Simmer for 10 minutes, stirring occasionally. Add the okra and mix well.
▼ Simmer for 10 minutes, stirring occasionally. Add the shrimp and mix well.
▼ Simmer for 5 minutes, stirring occasionally. Stir in the crab meat, filé powder and rice.
▼ Simmer just until heated through. Ladle into heated soup bowls. Serve immediately.

Okra is a must in gumbo. When cut, a gummy substance or soluble fiber seeps out and acts as a thickening agent. Filé powder is also used as a traditional thickening agent when preparing gumbo and is always added at the end of the cooking process. Most often found in gourmet stores, filé is ground sassafras root.

Per Serving: Calories 448; Total Fat 7 g; Saturated Fat 1 g; Cholesterol 223 mg; Sodium 544 mg; Carbohydrate 52 g; Fiber 7 g; Protein 43 g; Calcium 302 mg

Thai Curry Shrimp with Rice Noodle Chop Suey

Wine: French Gentil   Makes 4 servings

For the curry paste

1 teaspoon coriander seeds
1/2 teaspoon cumin seeds
1/2 teaspoon black peppercorns
4 poblano peppers, seeded
3 stalks lemon grass
2 tablespoons chopped shallots
1 tablespoon chopped gingerroot
1 tablespoon sesame oil
2 garlic cloves

For the chop suey

2 ounces mung bean threads (rice noodles)
1/2 cup julienned red bell pepper
2 garlic cloves, minced
1 tablespoon sesame oil
1/2 cup each julienned zucchini, carrot
    and scallions
4 ounces oyster sauce

For the shrimp

1 tablespoon sesame oil
24 large shrimp, peeled, deveined
1 cup evaporated skim milk

To prepare the curry paste

▼ Sauté the coriander seeds, cumin seeds and peppercorns in a skillet over medium heat for 5 minutes.
▼ Purée the coriander seed mixture and the remaining curry paste ingredients in a food processor; strain. Store, covered, in a plastic container in the refrigerator.

To prepare the chop suey

▼ Soak the mung beans in enough hot water to cover in a bowl for 30 minutes; drain.
▼ Sauté the red pepper and garlic in the sesame oil in a skillet over medium heat for 2 to 3 minutes. Stir in the zucchini, carrot and scallions.
▼ Sauté for 2 minutes longer. Add the oyster sauce and mung beans and mix well.
▼ Cook just until heated through, stirring constantly.

To prepare the shrimp

▼ Heat the sesame oil in a large skillet until hot. Stir in 1 heaping tablespoon of the curry paste. Sauté for 1 minute. Add the shrimp and mix well.
▼ Sauté for 2 minutes. Remove the shrimp to a platter. Stir in the evaporated milk.
▼ Cook until the liquid is reduced by 1/2, stirring constantly. Return the shrimp to the skillet and mix well. Cook just until heated through, stirring constantly.

To assemble

▼ Spoon the chop suey onto a heated platter. Top with the shrimp mixture.

 Curry, a highly seasoned sauce, is more often thought of as the powder in one's spice cabinet. Curries range in strength from fiercely hot to mild.

Per Serving: Calories 373; Total Fat 13 g; Saturated Fat 2 g; Cholesterol 162 mg; Sodium 1421 mg;
Carbohydrate 37 g; Fiber 3 g; Protein 29 g; Calcium 285 mg
Nutritional profile includes the entire amount of the curry paste.

Angel Hair Pasta with Shrimp and Peas

Wine: Italian Bianco di Custoza   Makes 4 servings

4 garlic cloves, chopped
2 tablespoons chopped shallots
2 tablespoons olive oil
1/4 cup chopped red bell pepper
8 ounces shrimp, peeled, deveined
1 cup vegetable stock
2 tablespoons chopped fresh basil
1 cup fresh peas
1 pound angel hair pasta, cooked, drained
3 tablespoons grated Parmesan cheese

Method of preparation

▼ Sauté the garlic and shallots in the olive oil in a skillet over medium heat for 2 to 3 minutes. Stir in the red pepper.
▼ Sauté for 3 to 4 minutes. Add the shrimp.
▼ Sauté for 3 to 4 minutes. Stir in the stock and basil. Bring to a simmer.
▼ Simmer for 4 to 5 minutes, stirring occasionally. Add the peas and mix well.
▼ Cook just until heated through, stirring frequently. Add the pasta, tossing to mix.
▼ Cook just until heated through, stirring frequently.
▼ Spoon the pasta mixture onto a heated serving platter. Sprinkle with the cheese. Serve immediately.

Shallots are considered a variety of onion but have a delicate flavor all their own. Sometimes mistaken for both scallions and garlic, they are often used in classical French sauces. When purchasing, look for firm bulbs with a paper-thin reddish skin. They will keep for several months if stored in a cool, well-ventilated location.

Per Serving: Calories 599; Total Fat 11 g; Saturated Fat 2 g; Cholesterol 89 mg; Sodium 165 mg; Carbohydrate 93 g; Fiber 5 g; Protein 30 g; Calcium 122 mg

Bow Tie Pasta with
Fava Beans and Pancetta

Wine: Vernaccia   Makes 4 servings

1/2 cup dried fava beans
2 cups water
1 pound bow tie pasta
5 ounces pancetta, cut into 1/8-inch pieces
1 cup chicken stock
1/2 cup chopped red tomato
5 garlic cloves, minced
3 tablespoons chopped fresh parsley
3 tablespoons chopped fresh basil
1/2 teaspoon red pepper flakes
Salt and black pepper to taste

Method of preparation

▼ Rinse and sort the fava beans. Combine the beans and water in a saucepan. Bring to a boil; reduce heat.
▼ Simmer the beans for 1 1/2 hours or until the beans are tender; do not drain.
▼ Cook the pasta using package directions; drain.
▼ Sauté the pancetta in a saucepan over medium heat until crisp. Add the undrained beans, stock, tomato, garlic, parsley, basil, red pepper flakes, salt and black pepper and mix well. Bring to a simmer, stirring occasionally. Add the pasta and mix gently.
▼ Cook just until heated through. Ladle into heated pasta bowls. Serve immediately.

Often used in Portuguese cooking, fava beans are quite large compared to other varieties of dried beans. Also called a broad bean, the fava is more widely available dried but also may be found canned. Like all legumes, they are a great source of protein, fiber, and complex carbohydrates.

Per Serving: Calories 619; Total Fat 6 g; Saturated Fat 1 g; Cholesterol 25 mg; Sodium 979 mg;
Carbohydrate 108 g; Fiber 6 g; Protein 33 g; Calcium 175 mg

Farfalle with Savory Ratatouille

Wine: California Sauvignon Blanc   Makes 4 servings

1 cup (¹/₈-inch pieces) eggplant
2 tablespoons olive oil
1 cup (¹/₈-inch pieces) zucchini
¹/₂ cup (¹/₈-inch pieces) yellow squash
¹/₂ cup (¹/₈-inch pieces) yellow bell pepper
¹/₂ cup (¹/₈-inch pieces) red bell pepper
1¹/₂ cups chopped red tomatoes
¹/₄ cup red wine
2 tablespoons chopped fresh basil
2 tablespoons chopped fresh parsley
2 tablespoons capers, rinsed, drained
1 pound farfalle, cooked, drained
3 tablespoons grated Parmesan cheese

Method of preparation

▼ Sauté the eggplant in the olive oil in a saucepan over medium heat for 3 to 4 minutes. Add the zucchini and yellow squash and mix well.
▼ Sauté for 3 to 4 minutes. Stir in the peppers.
▼ Sauté for 3 to 4 minutes longer; reduce heat. Add the tomatoes and red wine and mix well.
▼ Simmer for 10 to 15 minutes, stirring occasionally. Stir in the basil, parsley and capers.
▼ Simmer for 15 minutes, stirring occasionally. Remove from heat. Add the hot pasta and mix gently. Stir in the cheese.
▼ Spoon onto a heated serving platter. Serve immediately.

Tell your children they will be eating butterfly and vegetable stew for dinner and watch them flock to the table! Farfalle is a butterfly- or bow tie-shaped pasta, and ratatouille is a medley of seasoned vegetables. Whatever you decide to call this dish, it is pleasing to the eye, tantalizing on the tongue and, chock-full of nutritional value.

Per Serving: Calories 543; Total Fat 10 g; Saturated Fat 2 g; Cholesterol 3 mg; Sodium 126 mg; Carbohydrate 93 g; Fiber 5 g; Protein 8 g; Calcium 93 mg

Fettuccine with Sweet Peppers and Prosciutto

Wine: Alsatian Pinot Blanc   Makes 4 servings

1 pound fettuccine
1 cup julienned red bell pepper
1 cup julienned yellow bell pepper
$1/4$ cup chopped celery
3 garlic cloves, minced
2 tablespoons olive oil
4 ounces prosciutto, finely chopped
$1^1/2$ cups chicken stock
$1/4$ cup chopped fresh parsley
$1/2$ teaspoon red pepper flakes
Salt and black pepper to taste

Method of preparation
▼ Cook the fettuccine using package directions. Rinse the pasta in cold water and drain. Chill, covered, in a bowl in the refrigerator.
▼ Sauté the bell peppers, celery and garlic in the olive oil in a saucepan over medium heat for 7 to 8 minutes. Add the prosciutto and stock and mix well. Bring to a boil; reduce heat. Stir in the pasta.
▼ Simmer for 5 to 6 minutes, stirring frequently. Stir in the parsley, red pepper flakes, salt and black pepper.
▼ Spoon onto a heated serving platter. Serve immediately.

Fresh parsley is often overlooked as a nutritious addition to a recipe. One cup of chopped parsley provides a day's worth of vitamins A and C for only twenty-six calories. The curly variety is most often used since it is easy to chop and makes an attractive garnish. If you've had too much garlic, try munching on the parsley garnish as a natural breath freshener.

Per Serving: Calories 555; Total Fat 11 g; Saturated Fat 2 g; Cholesterol 20 mg; Sodium 782 mg; Carbohydrate 89 g; Fiber 4 g; Protein 23 g; Calcium 40 mg

Spinach Fettuccine á la Fresca

Wine: Orvieto   Makes 4 servings

1¹/₂ pounds spinach fettuccine
2 cups chopped red tomatoes
2 cups chopped yellow tomatoes
2 tablespoons garlic paste
2 tablespoons olive oil
2 tablespoons chopped fresh basil
1 tablespoon chopped fresh parsley
¹/₂ teaspoon red pepper flakes
Salt and black pepper to taste

Method of preparation

▼ Cook the pasta using package directions; drain.
▼ Combine the tomatoes, garlic paste, olive oil, basil, parsley, red pepper flakes, salt and black pepper in a bowl and mix well.
▼ Let stand at room temperature. Add the pasta and toss gently.
▼ Serve immediately.

Vegetable-flavored pastas do not contain enough vegetable to substitute for your salad or vegetable side dish, but they do add eye and taste appeal. The fettuccine noodle is very versatile, working best when topped with a sauce or when used in soups and salads. Store dry pasta in a cool, dry place and it will last indefinitely. Fresh pasta must be stored in the refrigerator.

Per Serving: Calories 737; Total Fat 12 g; Saturated Fat 2 g; Cholesterol 0 mg; Sodium 38 mg; Carbohydrate 137 g; Fiber 7 g; Protein 24 g; Calcium 100 mg

Fusilli with Fennel and Scallops

Wine: Pinot Grigio   Makes 4 servings

1 cup thinly sliced fennel
1 tablespoon olive oil
2 garlic cloves, minced
1 pound bay scallops
$1/2$ cup chopped tomato
2 tablespoons lemon juice
1 tablespoon anisette
1 teaspoon grated lemon zest
1 pound fusilli, cooked, drained
2 tablespoons grated Parmesan cheese

Method of preparation

▼ Sauté the fennel in the olive oil in a saucepan over medium heat for 2 to 3 minutes. Add the garlic and mix well.
▼ Sauté for 2 to 3 minutes longer. Stir in the scallops.
▼ Sauté for 5 to 6 minutes or until the scallops are tender. Stir in the tomato, lemon juice, anisette and lemon zest.
▼ Sauté for 1 minute.
▼ Spoon the hot pasta onto a heated serving platter. Top with the scallop mixture; sprinkle with the cheese.
▼ Serve immediately.

Fennel is a vegetable that tastes like licorice. Actually a member of the parsley family, fennel is often used in Italian and French cooking. The Italians tend to treat fennel as a vegetable, mostly using the bulb and stalks, while the French generally use the leaves as a seasoning. A great substitute for celery on the hors d'oeuvre tray.

Per Serving: Calories 592; Total Fat 7 g; Saturated Fat 1 g; Cholesterol 39 mg; Sodium 251 mg; Carbohydrate 93 g; Fiber 3 g; Protein 35 g; Calcium 98 mg

Fusilli with Swiss Chard and Feta Cheese

Wine: Pinot Grigio   Makes 4 servings

3 garlic cloves, minced
1 tablespoon olive oil
2 cups chopped tomatoes
2 pounds Swiss chard, chopped
1 pound fusilli, cooked, drained
Salt and pepper to taste
$1/2$ cup crumbled feta cheese

Method of preparation
▼ Sauté the garlic in the olive oil in a saucepan over medium heat for 1 minute. Add the tomatoes and mix well.
▼ Cook for 5 minutes, stirring occasionally. Stir in the Swiss chard.
▼ Steam, covered, for 5 minutes or until the Swiss chard is tender-crisp. Add the pasta, salt and pepper and mix gently.
▼ Spoon onto a heated serving platter. Sprinkle with the feta cheese.

Twisted spaghetti describes the fusilli variety of pasta. All pasta tastes best when cooked al dente, or to a consistency that is tender but firm. The only way to know if the pasta is done is to take a test bite. Always be careful to avoid overcooking.

Per Serving: Calories 554; Total Fat 9 g; Saturated Fat 3 g; Cholesterol 13 mg; Sodium 658 mg; Carbohydrate 99 g; Fiber 7 g; Protein 21 g; Calcium 215 mg

Chile Pepper Linguine Rustica

1 pound chile pepper linguine
$1/2$ cup chopped scallions
$1/4$ cup dry cured olives
5 garlic cloves, sliced
1 tablespoon olive oil
1 cup sliced shiitake mushrooms
Salt and pepper to taste

Method of preparation
▼ Cook the linguine using package directions; drain. Chill, covered, in a bowl in the refrigerator.
▼ Sauté the scallions, olives and garlic in the olive oil in a nonstick saucepan over medium heat for 2 to 3 minutes. Add the mushrooms and mix well.
▼ Sauté for 2 to 3 minutes or until the garlic is light brown. Add the pasta, tossing to mix.
▼ Sauté just until heated through. Season with salt and pepper.
▼ Spoon onto a heated serving platter. Serve immediately.

Shiitake mushrooms add excitement to this pasta dish. When preparing fresh mushrooms, avoid rinsing them. Simply brush or wipe them clean with a cloth. If using dried varieties, soak in water to cover for thirty minutes to four hours, drain and add to your favorite recipe. Mushrooms are a low-calorie addition to an entrée, and also provide a fair amount of fiber and potassium.

Per Serving: Calories 582; Total Fat 12 g; Saturated Fat 2 g; Cholesterol 0 mg; Sodium 824 mg; Carbohydrate 20 g; Fiber 7 g; Protein 2 g; Calcium 18 mg

Lemon Pepper Linguine with Spicy Lobster

Wine: French Pouilly-Fumé   Makes 4 servings

3 garlic cloves, minced
1 tablespoon olive oil
1 cup julienned red bell peppers
1 cup julienned yellow bell peppers
8 ounces shiitake mushrooms, julienned
8 ounces oyster mushrooms, julienned
1/2 cup chopped scallions
1 tablespoon minced jalapeño
1 pound lobster meat, chopped
1 1/2 cups chicken stock
2 tablespoons cornstarch
2 tablespoons white wine
1 pound lemon pepper linguine, cooked, drained
1/2 cup grated Parmesan cheese

Method of preparation

▼ Sauté the garlic in the olive oil in a saucepan for 2 to 3 minutes. Add the bell peppers, mushrooms, scallions and jalapeño and mix well.
▼ Sauté for 5 minutes. Stir in the lobster meat; reduce heat.
▼ Sauté for 2 to 3 minutes. Add the chicken stock and mix well. Bring to a simmer, stirring constantly. Stir in a mixture of the cornstarch and white wine.
▼ Cook just until thickened, stirring constantly. Add the pasta and toss gently.
▼ Spoon onto a heated serving platter. Sprinkle with the cheese. Serve immediately.

Did you know that it takes approximately seven years for a lobster to weigh one pound? Peak season for lobster is between May and September when harvesting occurs in North Atlantic waters. Lobsters should be purchased live and stored in the refrigerator, covered with a damp towel, to avoid the loss of moisture. Mild, sweet, and firm, lobster meat is protein-rich and virtually fat-free.

Per Serving: Calories 821; Total Fat 10 g; Saturated Fat 3 g; Cholesterol 116 mg; Sodium 596 mg; Carbohydrate 54 g; Fiber 12 g; Protein 49 g; Calcium 220 mg

Linguine with Fresh Herb Pesto and Roasted Tomatoes

Wine: Orvieto   Makes 4 servings

2 tablespoons olive oil
2 tablespoons chopped fresh basil
1 tablespoon chopped fresh oregano
1 tablespoon chopped fresh thyme
1 tablespoon chopped fresh sage
1 tablespoon chopped chives
3 garlic cloves, sliced
4 red tomatoes
1 teaspoon olive oil
1 pound linguine

Method of preparation
▼ Preheat the oven to 450 degrees.
▼ Combine 2 tablespoons olive oil, basil, oregano, thyme, sage, chives and garlic in a food processor container fitted with a steel blade. Process until smooth and of pesto consistency.
▼ Rub the tomatoes with 1 teaspoon olive oil. Arrange on a baking sheet.
▼ Bake for 15 minutes. Peel and chop the tomatoes, discarding the skins. Add the tomatoes to the pesto and mix well.
▼ Cook the pasta in a saucepan using package directions; drain. Return the pasta to the saucepan. Add the pesto and toss gently.

Worthy of being added to the "Seven Wonders of the World" list, pesto is bliss! Usually prepared with basil, this variation incorporates the flavors of several herbs and is virtually sodium-free. Experiment with what you have on hand for a personal twist. Make extra and freeze for future use in two-tablespoon portions in small freezer bags or in an ice cube tray.

Per Serving: Calories 523; Total Fat 10 g; Saturated Fat 1 g; Cholesterol 0 mg; Sodium 20 mg; Carbohydrate 92 g; Fiber 4 g; Protein 16 g; Calcium 50 mg

Baked Mostaccioli with Spicy Sausage

Wine: Pinot Grigio   Makes 4 servings

3 ounces sausage
3 garlic cloves, minced
1 teaspoon red pepper flakes
3 cups chopped tomatoes
4 ounces sliced mushrooms
1/4 cup red wine
1 tablespoon chopped fresh basil
1 teaspoon chopped fresh rosemary
1 pound mostaccioli, cooked, drained
1/3 cup part-skim milk ricotta cheese
1/2 cup fresh bread crumbs
1 teaspoon grated Parmesan cheese

Method of preparation
▼ Preheat the oven to 350 degrees.
▼ Brown the sausage in a skillet, stirring until crumbly. Stir in the garlic and red pepper flakes.
▼ Sauté for 2 minutes. Add the tomatoes, mushrooms, red wine, basil and rosemary and mix well. Bring to a simmer.
▼ Simmer for 15 to 20 minutes or until of the desired consistency, stirring occasionally. Combine with the pasta in a bowl and mix well. Spoon into a baking dish; dot with the ricotta cheese. Top with a mixture of the bread crumbs and Parmesan cheese.
▼ Bake for 20 minutes or until brown and bubbly.

How do you feed four people with three ounces of sausage? Use the sausage as a flavoring agent instead of as the center of the meal and you can can savor the taste without adding a large amount of fat or saturated fat. Omit the sausage to reduce the total fat grams to five and the saturated fat grams to two.

Per Serving: Calories 645; Total Fat 14 g; Saturated Fat 5 g; Cholesterol 21 mg; Sodium 292 mg; Carbohydrate 105 g; Fiber 5 g; Protein 23 g; Calcium 111 mg

Orecchiette with Caramelized Vidalia Onions

Wine: Chilean Sauvignon Blanc   Makes 4 servings

2 tablespoons butter
3 cups thinly sliced Vidalia onions
1 tablespoon sugar
1 cup vegetable stock
2 tablespoons chopped fresh parsley
1/2 teaspoon red pepper flakes
Salt and black pepper to taste
1 pound orecchiette, cooked, drained

Method of preparation

▼ Melt the butter in a large sauté pan over medium heat. Add the onions.
▼ Sauté for 15 to 20 minutes or just until the onions begin to brown; increase the heat. Stir in the sugar.
▼ Sauté until the onions are caramelized or dark brown. Add the stock. Bring to a simmer.
▼ Simmer for 3 to 4 minutes, stirring frequently. Stir in the parsley, red pepper flakes, salt and black pepper. Add the pasta and mix gently.
▼ Cook just until heated through, stirring frequently.
▼ Spoon into heated pasta bowls. Serve immediately.

This ear-shaped pasta captures the fantastic juices of the caramelized onions and delivers them to your palate with a fanfare. Although any onion will do, the Vidalia is preferred for its sweet flavor. The browning or caramelizing of the onions brings out the taste of a lifetime and is bound to turn an onion loather into an onion lover.

Per Serving: Calories 509; Total Fat 8 g; Saturated Fat 4 g; Cholesterol 15 mg; Sodium 512 mg; Carbohydrate 93 g; Fiber 5 g; Protein 16 g; Calcium 81 mg

Penne with Broccoli Rabe and Spicy Red Pepper Oil

Wine: Vernaccia   Makes 4 servings

4 garlic cloves, minced
1 tablespoon olive oil
1 cup chopped red bell pepper
1 1/2 teaspoons red pepper flakes
1 1/2 pounds broccoli rabe, trimmed, chopped
1 pound penne
1/4 cup grated Parmesan cheese

Method of preparation
▼ Sauté the garlic in the olive oil in a skillet over medium heat for 2 to 3 minutes. Add the red pepper, red pepper flakes and rabe and mix well.
▼ Sauté for 5 to 6 minutes.
▼ Cook the pasta using package directions. Drain, reserving 1/2 cup of the liquid.
▼ Combine the reserved liquid, pasta and rabe mixture in a saucepan and toss gently. Cook for 1 minute, stirring frequently.
▼ Spoon onto a heated serving platter. Sprinkle with the cheese. Serve immediately.

Rabe, or leaves of the broccoli plant, contains a bonanza of beta-carotene. Also known as an antioxidant, this plant form which is rich in vitamin A is showing promising results as having a role in the prevention of cancer. Slightly bitter in taste, rabe is popular in Italian cuisine.

Per Serving: Calories 533; Total Fat 7 g; Saturated Fat 2 g; Cholesterol 4 mg; Sodium 102 mg; Carbohydrate 96 g; Fiber 5 g; Protein 22 g; Calcium 516 mg

Chile Pepper Penne in Scallop Sauce

Wine: Pinot Blanc   Makes 4 servings

3/4 cup chopped onion
4 garlic cloves, minced
2 tablespoons olive oil
12 ounces bay scallops, sliced
3 cups chopped red tomatoes
1/2 cup white wine
1 tablespoon chopped fresh basil
1 tablespoon chopped fresh parsley
1/2 teaspoon red pepper flakes
Salt and black pepper to taste
1 pound chile pepper penne, cooked, drained

Method of preparation
▼ Sauté the onion and garlic in the olive oil in a saucepan over medium heat for 3 to 4 minutes. Add the scallops and mix well.
▼ Sauté for 1 minute. Stir in the tomatoes and white wine. Bring to a boil; reduce heat.
▼ Simmer for 10 to 12 minutes, stirring occasionally. Add the basil, parsley, red pepper flakes, salt and black pepper and mix well. Add the pasta and toss gently.
▼ Cook over medium heat for 1 minute, stirring frequently.
▼ Spoon onto a heated serving platter. Serve immediately.

Scallops are actually a muscle. Their sweet taste is due to glycogen, a stored form of carbohydrate generally found in muscle. The bay variety is considered to be more tender and tastier than the sea scallop.

Per Serving: Calories 615; Total Fat 10 g; Saturated Fat 1 g; Cholesterol 28 mg; Sodium 271 mg; Carbohydrate 96 g; Fiber 5 g; Protein 30 g; Calcium 72 mg

Porcini Penne with Goat Cheese

Wine: Gavi   Makes 4 servings

1 cup evaporated skim milk
4 ounces goat cheese
3 tablespoons grated Parmesan cheese
1 pound porcini penne, cooked, drained
1 tablespoon chopped fresh dillweed
1 tablespoon chopped fresh basil
1 teaspoon chopped fresh parsley
Salt and pepper to taste

Method of preparation
▼ Bring the evaporated milk, goat cheese and Parmesan cheese to a simmer in a
   saucepan, stirring constantly. Remove from heat.
▼ Add the pasta, dillweed, basil, parsley, salt and pepper and toss gently.
▼ Spoon onto a heated serving platter. Serve immediately.

This dish is a calcium extravaganza, providing 50 percent of the daily
recommendation. Great news, since the risk for developing osteoporosis can
be reduced by including calcium-rich foods in one's diet. If you're not interested
in goat cheese or want to lower the fat content, try your favorite low-fat cheese. Just
don't skip the cheese . . . it tastes great and keeps the bones strong and healthy.

Per Serving: Calories 617; Total Fat 13 g; Saturated Fat 3 g; Cholesterol 35 mg; Sodium 263 mg;
Carbohydrate 96 g; Fiber 0 g; Protein 29 g; Calcium 504 mg

Tomato Basil Penne with Cranberry Beans

Wine: Chianti   Makes 4 servings

1 cup dried cranberry beans
4 cups water
4 ounces pancetta, cut into $1/8$-inch pieces
$1/2$ cup chopped red onion
2 garlic cloves, minced
2 cups chicken stock
1 teaspoon chili powder
6 ounces spinach, chopped
$11/2$ tablespoons cornstarch
$1/3$ cup white wine
8 ounces tomato basil penne, cooked, drained
3 ounces Parmesan cheese, grated

Method of preparation

▼ Sort and rinse the cranberry beans. Combine the beans with enough water to cover in a bowl. Let stand for 8 to 10 hours; drain.
▼ Combine the beans and 4 cups water in a saucepan. Bring to a boil.
▼ Simmer for $11/2$ hours or until tender; drain.
▼ Fry the pancetta in a saucepan over medium heat until crisp. Add the red onion and garlic and mix well.
▼ Sauté for 2 to 3 minutes. Stir in the stock and chili powder. Bring to a boil; reduce heat.
▼ Simmer for 2 to 3 minutes, stirring occasionally. Add the spinach and mix well.
▼ Simmer for 1 to 2 minutes, stirring occasionally.
▼ Dissolve the cornstarch in the white wine in a bowl. Add to the spinach mixture and mix well.
▼ Cook until thickened, stirring constantly. Stir in the cranberry beans. Add the pasta and mix gently.
▼ Spoon onto a heated platter. Sprinkle with the cheese. Serve immediately.

Pancetta is a delightfully flavored cured pork product. Lean by comparison to many processed meats, it is very high in sodium. Canned broths, although labeled low-sodium, are extremely high in sodium as well. Reduce the amount of sodium in this recipe by using salt-free homemade chicken stock and less pancetta.

Per Serving: Calories 586; Total Fat 11 g; Saturated Fat 5 g; Cholesterol 37 mg; Sodium 1213 mg; Carbohydrate 82 g; Fiber 16 g; Protein 38 g; Calcium 439 mg

Pennette with Eggplant and Tomatoes

Wine: Bianco di Custoza   Makes 4 servings

1/4 cup sun-dried tomatoes
2 cups (1/4-inch slices) Japanese eggplant
4 garlic cloves, minced
2 tablespoons olive oil
2 cups chopped red tomatoes
1/2 teaspoon red pepper flakes
1/4 cup chopped fresh basil
Chopped fresh parsley to taste
1 pound pennette, cooked, drained

Method of preparation

▼ Soak the sun-dried tomatoes in water to cover in a bowl; drain.
▼ Sauté the eggplant and garlic in the olive oil in a saucepan over medium heat for 5 to 6 minutes. Stir in the sun-dried tomatoes, red tomatoes and red pepper flakes. Bring to a simmer.
▼ Simmer for 15 to 20 minutes, stirring occasionally. Stir in the basil and parsley.
▼ Toss the pasta with the sauce in a bowl. Spoon onto a heated serving platter. Serve immediately.

Eating "real" foods for nourishment still remains the preferred method over pills, since scientists are discovering the natural disease-fighting properties of substances found only in foods. One such substance is lycopene, which recent studies have linked with the prevention of certain cancers. Cooked tomatoes may offer this protection, as lycopene is not destroyed by heating.

Per Serving: Calories 525; Total Fat 9 g; Saturated Fat 1 g; Cholesterol 0 mg; Sodium 88 mg; Carbohydrate 94 g; Fiber 5 g; Protein 16 g; Calcium 41 mg

Radiatore with Sausage and Roasted Red Peppers

Wine: Alsatian Pinot Blanc   Makes 4 servings

1 1/2 pounds radiatore
5 red bell peppers
4 ounces Italian sausage
6 garlic cloves, minced
1/4 cup chopped onion
1 cup chicken stock
1 cup chopped red tomatoes
3 ears corn, roasted, scraped
2 tablespoons chopped fresh basil
1 tablespoon chopped fresh parsley
Salt and pepper to taste

Method of preparation

▼ Preheat the oven to 450 degrees.
▼ Cook the pasta using package directions. Drain and rinse with cold water.
▼ Place the red peppers on a baking sheet. Roast for 10 to 15 minutes or until blackened. Place the peppers in a sealable plastic bag. Seal the bag.
▼ Let stand for 15 to 20 minutes or until cool. Peel and seed the peppers; cut into 1/2-inch slices.
▼ Brown the sausage in a saucepan over medium heat, stirring until crumbly. Add the garlic and mix well.
▼ Sauté for 2 to 3 minutes. Stir in the onion.
▼ Sauté for 5 minutes longer. Stir in the stock and tomatoes. Bring to a boil; reduce heat.
▼ Simmer for 5 minutes, stirring occasionally. Add the corn, basil, parsley, salt and pepper and mix well. Add the pasta and mix gently.
▼ Cook just until heated through, stirring frequently.
▼ Spoon the pasta onto a heated platter; top with the roasted red peppers. Serve immediately.

Roasting corn is easy. Simply remove the husks and silk. Next, brush the kernels with a little olive oil or spray with nonstick cooking spray. Arrange the ears on a baking sheet and bake at 400 degrees for 15 minutes or until light brown. Delicious and nutritious!

Per Serving: Calories 347; Total Fat 11 g; Saturated Fat 3 g; Cholesterol 22 mg; Sodium 268 mg; Carbohydrate 52 g; Fiber 6 g; Protein 13 g; Calcium 98 mg

Rigatoni alla Ragù

Wine: Sauvignon Blanc   Makes 4 servings

1 pound rigatoni
3 garlic cloves, minced
1 tablespoon olive oil
12 ounces ground veal
$^1/_2$ cup minced onion
$^1/_4$ cup minced celery
$^1/_4$ cup minced carrot
$^1/_4$ cup minced leek
$^1/_4$ cup red wine
2 cups chopped red tomatoes
1 cup chicken stock
2 tablespoons chopped fresh parsley
Salt and pepper to taste

Method of preparation
▼ Cook the pasta using package directions. Drain and rinse in cold water. Chill, covered, in the refrigerator.
▼ Sauté the garlic in the olive oil in a saucepan over medium heat for 2 minutes. Add the veal.
▼ Cook until the veal is brown, stirring constantly. Add the onion, celery, carrot and leek and mix well.
▼ Cook for 10 to 12 minutes or until the vegetables are tender, stirring occasionally. Stir in the red wine.
▼ Cook for 3 to 4 minutes, stirring occasionally. Add the tomatoes and stock and mix well.
▼ Simmer for 20 to 25 minutes or until thickened, stirring occasionally. Stir in the parsley, salt and pepper. Add the pasta and toss gently.
▼ Spoon onto a heated serving platter. Serve immediately.

Break your meat sauce paradigm by using ground veal instead of ground beef. You will experience a new flavor and save seventy-seven calories and nine grams of fat per serving. The other good news is that while reducing calories and fat, you will be consuming four of the six-to-eleven daily recommended servings from the grain group.

Per Serving: Calories 625; Total Fat 11 g; Saturated Fat 3 g; Cholesterol 70 mg; Sodium 173 mg; Carbohydrate 94 g; Fiber 5 g; Protein 33 g; Calcium 64 mg

Imagine a musical masterpiece that suddenly
loses the entire violin section . . . a disaster to the total
beauty of the work. Think of your meal as a
symphony, its enjoyment dependent on the nuances of
different instruments. Just like music, your accompaniments
provide a voice that adds to the dynamic nature
of the eating experience as well.

A mound of peas or a bed of unadorned noodles.
These are the old paradigms of side-dish offerings. Expand
your horizons by serving a pancake, relish, beans,
or grains to complement your entrée. Think about the excitement
created by serving Grilled Flank Steak with Red Wine
Sauce alongside Crispy Potato Galette and Asparagus with
Lemon Relish. A perfect pairing is Roasted Catfish with Caramelized
Onions and New Orleans Red Beans and Rice. And who could
not enjoy the delicate flavors of Ballotine of Baby Chicken
served with Barley and Wild Mushroom Pilaf.

Go ahead and experiment. Put on your paradigm-busting
hat and match items that simply sound appealing to
you. The combinations are limited only by your imagination.

COMPLEMENTS

™

SIDE DISHES

Asparagus with Lemon Relish

Makes 4 servings

For the lemon relish

3 anchovies
1 cup chopped scallions
1/4 cup chopped fresh parsley
1 tablespoon grated lemon zest
3 tablespoons lemon juice
2 teaspoons olive oil

For the asparagus

1 1/2 pounds asparagus, trimmed

To prepare the lemon relish
▼ Mash the anchovies in a bowl until of a paste consistency.
▼ Combine the scallions, parsley and lemon zest in a bowl and mix well. Stir in a mixture of the lemon juice and olive oil. Add the anchovies and mix well.

To prepare the asparagus
▼ Divide the asparagus into 2 portions; tie each portion with kitchen twine.
▼ Bring a small amount of water to boil in a saucepan. Add the asparagus.
▼ Steam, covered, for 4 to 5 minutes or until the asparagus is tender-crisp; drain.

To assemble
▼ Arrange the asparagus with tips facing outward on a round serving platter. Sprinkle the lemon relish over the asparagus.
▼ Serve immediately.

Choose your asparagus carefully. The spears should be round, straight, and of uniform thickness, with tight pointed tips that have not yet started to flower. Flat angular stalks are usually tough. A good source of potassium, vitamin A, iron, and folate, the quality is best when the asparagus is used as soon as possible after purchase. Wrap in a damp towel, place in a sealable plastic bag, and store in the refrigerator for a few days at the most.

Per Serving: Calories 84; Total Fat 3 g; Saturated Fat 0 g; Cholesterol 2 mg; Sodium 28 mg; Carbohydrate 13 g; Fiber 5 g; Protein 6 g; Calcium 116 mg

Black Beans with Saffron Rice

Makes 4 servings

For the salsa

2 cups chopped red tomatoes
1 cup chopped scallions
2 tablespoons chopped fresh mint
1 tablespoon lime juice
1 teaspoon cumin
$1/4$ teaspoon cayenne

For the beans and rice

1 cup cooked black beans
$1^1/2$ cups vegetable stock
$3/4$ cup rice
$1/2$ cup finely chopped onion
4 garlic cloves, minced
2 bay leaves
$1/4$ teaspoon saffron

To prepare the salsa

▼ Combine the tomatoes, scallions, mint, lime juice, cumin and cayenne in a bowl and mix well.

To prepare the beans and rice

▼ Rinse and drain the black beans in a colander.
▼ Combine the stock, rice, onion, garlic, bay leaves and saffron in a saucepan and mix well. Bring to a boil; reduce heat.
▼ Simmer, covered, for 20 minutes or until the broth has been absorbed and the rice is tender. Discard the bay leaves.

To assemble

▼ Spoon the rice onto a heated serving platter. Top with the black beans and salsa.

Proteins from plant and vegetable sources are called incomplete proteins because they are usually lacking sufficient amounts of one or more of the essential amino acids (protein building blocks). When two incomplete proteins are combined in one meal, they produce complete protein if the right foods are chosen and eaten in the correct amounts. This combination of beans and rice combines to provide the body with delicious complete protein!

Per Serving: Calories 227; Total Fat 1 g; Saturated Fat 0 g; Cholesterol 0 mg; Sodium 91 mg; Carbohydrate 47 g; Fiber 7 g; Protein 8 g; Calcium 75 mg

New Orleans Red Beans and Rice

Makes 4 servings

1/2 cup dried red kidney beans
3 cups water
3 ounces andouille sausage
1/2 cup chopped onion
1/4 cup chopped celery
2 garlic cloves, minced
1 cup chicken stock
1 teaspoon chopped fresh thyme
1/4 teaspoon cayenne
2 cups hot cooked rice

Method of preparation

▼ Sort and rinse the kidney beans. Combine with enough water to cover in a bowl. Let stand for 8 to 10 hours; drain.
▼ Combine the beans with 3 cups water in a saucepan. Bring to a boil; reduce heat.
▼ Simmer over medium heat for 1 1/4 hours or until tender, stirring occasionally; drain.
▼ Brown the sausage in a saucepan. Add the onion, celery and garlic and mix well.
▼ Sauté for 4 minutes or until the vegetables are tender. Stir in the stock, thyme and cayenne. Bring to a boil; reduce heat.
▼ Simmer for 5 to 6 minutes, stirring occasionally. Stir in the kidney beans. Add the rice and mix well.
▼ Simmer for 5 minutes longer, stirring frequently. Serve immediately.

Traditional noonday fare in New Orleans on Mondays, kidney beans are also an integral part of meals from New England to Central America. One of the most popular legumes, kidney beans are renowned for their protein and fiber but also contain considerable amounts of potassium and folate. By soaking the beans overnight, some of the sugars that cause gas are leached into the water, which is then drained before cooking.

Per Serving: Calories 308; Total Fat 9 g; Saturated Fat 3 g; Cholesterol 14 mg; Sodium 228 mg; Carbohydrate 45 g; Fiber 4 g; Protein 11 g; Calcium 51 mg

Sautéed Beet Greens with Shallots

Makes 4 servings

1¹/2 pounds beet greens
4 cups water
¹/4 cup minced shallots
1 tablespoon butter
2 tablespoons balsamic vinegar
¹/4 teaspoon red pepper flakes
Salt and black pepper to taste

Method of preparation
▼ Trim the stems from the beet greens.
▼ Bring the water to a boil in a saucepan and add the beet greens; reduce heat.
▼ Simmer for 3 minutes; drain. Immerse the greens in cold water in a bowl. Drain the greens and squeeze out the moisture.
▼ Sauté the shallots in the butter in a saucepan over medium heat for 5 to 6 minutes or until brown. Stir in the balsamic vinegar and red pepper flakes.
▼ Cook until the liquid is reduced by ¹/2, stirring frequently. Add the beet greens and mix well.
▼ Cook just until heated through. Season with salt and black pepper.
▼ Spoon onto a heated platter. Serve immediately.

The greens of fresh beets are often discarded, and what a shame, for they are an excellent source of vitamin A. Ironically, the Romans ate only the beet greens and used the roots for medicinal purposes. The tops are fairly perishable so use them within two days after purchase. The potassium-rich tuber, or beet, can be stored in the vegetable crisper in the refrigerator for approximately two weeks.

Per Serving: Calories 66; Total Fat 3 g; Saturated Fat 2 g; Cholesterol 8 mg; Sodium 372 mg; Carbohydrate 9 g; Fiber 6 g; Protein 3 g; Calcium 208 mg

Grilled Polenta with Sun-Dried Tomatoes and Gorgonzola Cheese

Makes 4 servings

3 cups chicken stock
1 1/4 cups yellow cornmeal
2 ounces Gorgonzola cheese, crumbled
1/4 cup chopped drained sun-dried tomatoes
1/4 teaspoon freshly ground pepper

Method of preparation

▼ Bring the stock to a boil in a saucepan; reduce heat. Pour the cornmeal in a steady stream into the stock, stirring constantly.
▼ Cook for 5 minutes, stirring constantly. Remove from heat. Stir in the cheese, sun-dried tomatoes and pepper.
▼ Spread the polenta in a 9x9-inch dish lined with foil. Chill for 1 hour.
▼ Preheat the grill.
▼ Invert the polenta onto a flat surface. Cut into 3x3-inch diamond-shape portions. Spray both sides of the polenta with olive oil-flavor nonstick cooking spray.
▼ Grill 5 inches above hot coals for 4 minutes; turn. Grill for 4 minutes longer or until light brown.
▼ Arrange on a heated serving platter. Serve warm.

Polenta is an Italian version of cornmeal mush or grits cooked in stock. Cornmeal is made from field corn, which has more starch and less sugar than sweet corn. Available in yellow and white varieties, cornmeal of the yellow variety is richer in vitamin A.

Per Serving: Calories 227; Total Fat 5 g; Saturated Fat 3 g; Cholesterol 12 mg; Sodium 329 mg; Carbohydrate 36 g; Fiber 4 g; Protein 8 g; Calcium 82 mg

Crispy Potato Galette

Makes 4 servings

1 pound potatoes, peeled, sliced
2 teaspoons butter
1/2 cup buttermilk
1/2 cup shredded zucchini
1/2 cup chopped tomato
1/4 cup chopped scallions
2 tablespoons chopped basil
1/8 teaspoon nutmeg
Salt and pepper to taste
1/2 cup seasoned dry bread crumbs
2 tablespoons grated Parmesan cheese

Method of Preparation

▼ Combine the potatoes with enough water to cover in a saucepan. Cook over high heat for 45 minutes or until tender; drain.
▼ Combine the potatoes with the butter in a bowl and mash until blended. Stir in the buttermilk, zucchini, tomato, scallions, basil, nutmeg, salt and pepper. Shape into four 1-inch thick pancakes. Coat both sides with the bread crumbs.
▼ Preheat the oven to 350 degrees.
▼ Heat a large skillet sprayed with nonstick cooking spray over medium heat until hot.
▼ Cook the pancakes in the skillet until brown on both sides. Arrange on a baking sheet; sprinkle with the cheese.
▼ Bake for 10 to 12 minutes. Remove to a heated platter. Serve immediately.

A galette is a crispy potato pancake usually made with puréed potatoes. This recipe could be used for traditional croquettes but is much lower in fat when prepared as described. If using the thin-skinned new or red potato, leave on the skin, which provides extra fiber.

Per Serving: Calories 160; Total Fat 3 g; Saturated Fat 2 g; Cholesterol 8 mg; Sodium 135 mg; Carbohydrate 28 g; Fiber 3 g; Protein 6 g; Calcium 137 mg

Spicy Buttermilk Potatoes

Makes 4 servings

1¹/2 pounds potatoes, peeled, sliced
¹/2 cup nonfat sour cream
¹/3 cup buttermilk
2 tablespoons chopped fresh cilantro
2 tablespoons salsa
1 teaspoon chili powder
Salt and pepper to taste

Method of preparation
▼ Combine the potatoes with enough water to cover in a saucepan. Bring to a boil; reduce heat.
▼ Simmer for 45 minutes or until the potatoes are tender; drain. Press the potatoes through a ricer into a bowl.
▼ Preheat the oven to 350 degrees.
▼ Combine the sour cream, buttermilk, cilantro, salsa, chili powder, salt and pepper in a bowl and mix well. Stir in the potatoes. Spoon into a baking dish.
▼ Bake for 30 minutes or until golden brown.

Buttermilk, contrary to its name, is actually made from skim or low-fat milk. A bacterial culture is added to ferment the milk sugar, or lactose. The result is a thick, buttery-tasting product with little or no fat. If buttermilk is not available, combine one tablespoon lemon juice and one cup any type milk for an acceptable substitute.

Per Serving: Calories 183; Total Fat 1 g; Saturated Fat 0 g; Cholesterol 6 mg; Sodium 69 mg; Carbohydrate 38 g; Fiber 3 g; Protein 6 g; Calcium 38 mg

Apple and Onion Potato Pancakes

Makes 4 servings

1 1/2 pounds baking potatoes, peeled, shredded
2 Granny Smith apples, peeled, shredded
1 red onion, finely chopped
2 tablespoons minced fresh parsley
1/4 cup flour
1 teaspoon baking powder
1/4 teaspoon salt
1/8 teaspoon nutmeg
1/8 teaspoon cinnamon
2 eggs, beaten

Method of preparation
▼ Preheat the oven to 375 degrees.
▼ Combine the potatoes, apples, red onion and parsley in a bowl and mix well. Stir in a mixture of the flour, baking powder, salt, nutmeg, cinnamon and eggs.
▼ Let stand for 15 minutes.
▼ Heat a nonstick skillet sprayed with nonstick cooking spray over medium heat until hot. Drop the potato batter by spoonfuls into the prepared skillet and spread into 4-inch rounds; will yield approximately 12 pancakes.
▼ Cook for 3 minutes on each side. Arrange on a baking sheet.
▼ Bake for 6 to 7 minutes. Place on a heated serving platter. Serve immediately.

The potato has long been a staple in many cuisines and is considered a good source of vitamins and minerals. Dietary goals suggest that over half of the calories we eat on a daily basis should come from complex carbohydrates, which the potato contains in significant amounts. Store potatoes in a cool, dark, well-ventilated location, but do not refrigerate.

Per Serving: Calories 253; Total Fat 3 g; Saturated Fat 1 g; Cholesterol 106 mg; Sodium 277 mg; Carbohydrate 50 g; Fiber 5 g; Protein 9 g; Calcium 149 mg

Roasted Corn and Rice Pancakes
Makes 4 servings

2 ears corn, shucked
1 tablespoon melted margarine
1 cup skim milk
3/4 cup flour
1/4 teaspoon baking powder
1 egg, beaten
1/2 cup cooked brown rice
1/4 cup chopped scallions
1/4 cup (1/8-inch pieces) red bell pepper
1 tablespoon Dijon mustard
1 tablespoon chopped fresh parsley

Method of preparation
▼ Preheat the oven to 400 degrees.
▼ Brush the corn with the margarine. Place on a baking sheet.
▼ Roast for 15 minutes, turning occasionally. Let stand until cool.
▼ Combine the skim milk, flour, baking powder and egg in a bowl and mix well. Stir in the brown rice, scallions, red pepper, Dijon mustard and parsley. Scrape the corn kernels with a sharp knife into the batter and mix well.
▼ Heat a skillet sprayed with nonstick cooking spray until hot. Drop the batter by tablespoonfuls into the skillet. Cook until light brown on both sides, turning once or twice. Place the pancakes on a baking sheet and keep warm until serving time.
▼ Arrange on a heated platter. Serve immediately.

Looking for something a little unusual to serve with poultry or fish? These pancakes complete the entrée all by themselves as they contain a grain and several vegetables. Roasting brings out the corn's natural sweet flavors. Canned corn may be substituted, but using fresh corn is well worth the effort.

Per Serving: Calories 220; Total Fat 5 g; Saturated Fat 1 g; Cholesterol 54 mg; Sodium 162 mg; Carbohydrate 36 g; Fiber 2 g; Protein 8 g; Calcium 133 mg

Barley and Wild Mushroom Pilaf

Makes 4 servings

1/2 ounce dried porcini mushrooms
1/4 cup hot water
1/4 cup chopped onion
1/4 cup chopped celery
1 tablespoon butter
5 ounces barley
1 1/2 cups chicken stock
Salt and pepper to taste

Method of preparation

▼ Preheat the oven to 325 degrees.
▼ Combine the mushrooms and hot water in a bowl. Let stand for 10 minutes.
▼ Sauté the onion and celery in the butter in a Dutch oven over medium heat for 3 to 4 minutes. Stir in the barley.
▼ Sauté for 5 minutes. Add the stock and undrained mushrooms and mix well.
▼ Bake, covered, for 55 minutes or until the liquid has been absorbed. Fluff the pilaf with a fork; season with salt and pepper.
▼ Spoon onto a heated platter. Serve immediately.

Barley has had many uses throughout the centuries: currency, jewelry, burn salve, liquor, fermentation, and breakfast cereal. The majority of barley grown today is used as animal feed and in beer production. Coronary heart disease is rare in areas of the world where barley is a significant dietary staple.

Per Serving: Calories 167; Total Fat 4 g; Saturated Fat 2 g; Cholesterol 8 mg; Sodium 78 mg; Carbohydrate 29 g; Fiber 7 g; Protein 5 g; Calcium 21 mg

Brown Rice Pilaf

Makes 4 servings

2 cups chicken stock
1/2 cup long grain brown rice
1/3 cup wild rice
1/2 cup sliced mushrooms
1/4 cup chopped red bell pepper
1/4 cup chopped yellow bell pepper
1/4 cup chopped carrot
1/8 teaspoon curry powder
1/8 teaspoon pepper
1/8 teaspoon cumin
2 garlic cloves, minced
1 teaspoon olive oil

Method of preparation

▼ Bring the stock, brown rice and wild rice to a boil in a saucepan; reduce heat.
▼ Simmer, covered, for 55 minutes or until the liquid has been absorbed and the rice is tender.
▼ Sauté the mushrooms, bell peppers, carrot, curry powder, pepper, cumin and garlic in the olive oil in a skillet for 2 to 3 minutes. Add to the rice and mix gently.
▼ Spoon into a heated serving bowl. Serve immediately.

Wild rice is the seed of an aquatic grass and technically not rice at all. Since wild rice is never refined and the whole grain is cooked, it is rich in fiber, protein, B vitamins, and minerals. If watching cost, the less expensive medium grain or extra-fancy variety is a good substitute.

Per Serving: Calories 157; Total Fat 2 g; Saturated Fat 0 g; Cholesterol 0 mg; Sodium 6 mg; Carbohydrate 30 g; Fiber 2 g; Protein 5 g; Calcium 16 mg

Cilantro Pilaf

Makes 4 servings

2 serrano peppers, minced
1 garlic clove, minced
1 tablespoon olive oil
2 cups chicken stock
1 1/4 cups short grain rice
1/2 cup chopped tomatillos
1/2 cup chopped scallions
1/4 cup chopped fresh cilantro

Method of preparation

▼ Sauté the peppers and garlic in the olive oil in a saucepan over medium heat for 2 to 3 minutes. Stir in the stock, rice, tomatillos and scallions and cover. Bring to a boil; reduce heat.

▼ Simmer for 20 minutes or until the liquid has been absorbed. Stir in the cilantro and fluff with a fork.

▼ Spoon onto a heated serving platter. Serve immediately.

Once tested by human mouths (ouch!), chiles are now chemically categorized based on their level of capsaicin. Serrano peppers rate a six out of ten on the Official Chile Heat Scale. A proven antidote for the burning sensation of chiles is dairy products such as milk, sour cream, yogurt, or ice cream, which should be consumed immediatley. Casein, a protein in these products, acts as a detergent and literally washes away the capsaicin.

Per Serving: Calories 287; Total Fat 4 g; Saturated Fat 1 g; Cholesterol 0 mg; Sodium 9 mg; Carbohydrate 56 g; Fiber 3 g; Protein 6 g; Calcium 43 mg

Confetti Quinoa Pilaf

Makes 4 servings

1 tablespoon minced shallot
1 garlic clove, minced
2 teaspoons olive oil
4 ounces quinoa
1 cup chicken stock
1/4 cup chopped red bell pepper
1/4 cup chopped green bell pepper
1/4 cup yellow bell pepper
1 bay leaf

Method of preparation

▼ Preheat the oven to 350 degrees.
▼ Sauté the shallot and garlic in the olive oil in a Dutch oven for 2 minutes. Add the quinoa and mix well. Stir in the stock, bell peppers and bay leaf and cover. Bring to a boil, stirring frequently.
▼ Bake for 15 minutes. Discard the bay leaf. Fluff with a fork.

Quinoa (KEEN-wah) is a delicious grain, light and fluffy, and can be substituted for rice in many of the same dishes in which rice is an ingredient. Once the sacred staple of the Incas, and still commonly used in the South American cuisine, it is an exceptional source of iron and a quality source of protein.

Per Serving: Calories 136; Total Fat 4 g; Saturated Fat 1 g; Cholesterol 0 mg; Sodium 7 mg; Carbohydrate 22 g; Fiber 2 g; Protein 4 g; Calcium 25 mg

Risotto with Sun-Dried Tomatoes

Makes 4 servings

2 cups boiling water
1 ounce sun-dried tomatoes
2 cups sliced leeks
1 teaspoon olive oil
1 cup chopped red tomatoes
2 tablespoons chopped fresh parsley
1 tablespoon chopped fresh basil
Salt and pepper to taste
3 1/2 cups chicken stock
1 cup uncooked arborio rice

Method of preparation

▼ Combine the boiling water and sun-dried tomatoes in a bowl. Let stand for 5 minutes. Drain and set aside.
▼ Sauté the leeks in the olive oil in a skillet over medium heat for 5 minutes or until tender. Add the red tomatoes, parsley, basil, salt and pepper and mix well.
▼ Sauté for 2 to 3 minutes.
▼ Bring 2 cups of the stock to a boil in a saucepan; reduce heat.
▼ Stir in the rice.
▼ Simmer for 8 to 10 minutes or until most of the liquid has been absorbed, stirring constantly. Add the remaining stock and mix well.
▼ Simmer for 10 to 12 minutes longer or until the liquid has been absorbed and the rice is tender; the mixture will be creamy. Stir in the sun-dried tomatoes and leek mixture.
▼ Serve immediately.

Chinese food comes to mind when rice is mentioned, but the Italians are immense fans of the world's third-highest-produced grain. White rice provides fewer vitamins, minerals, and fiber than the brown variety, but both contain minimal fat and sodium. Arborio is the variety of rice traditionally used in risotto. If necessary, a short grain or round rice that tends to stick together after cooking is an acceptable substitute.

Per Serving: Calories 277; Total Fat 2 g; Saturated Fat 0 g; Cholesterol 0 mg; Sodium 183 mg; Carbohydrate 57 g; Fiber 3 g; Protein 8 g; Calcium 102 mg

Braised Swiss Chard with Sweet Blackberry Ginger Vinegar

Makes 4 servings

1 cup sliced Vidalia onion
2 garlic cloves, minced
1 1/2 tablespoons olive oil
1 1/2 pounds Swiss chard, chopped
3 tablespoons blackberry ginger vinegar (see page 166)
Salt and pepper to taste

Method of preparation

▼ Sauté the onion and garlic in the olive oil in a saucepan over medium heat for 3 to 4 minutes. Add the Swiss chard and blackberry ginger vinegar and mix well; reduce heat.
▼ Steam, covered, for 5 to 7 minutes or until the Swiss chard is tender. Season with salt and pepper.
▼ Serve immediately.

Nutritious, yet underused, Swiss chard is a type of beet grown for its leaves instead of its root. Its beta-carotene, which is turned into vitamin A in the body, and vitamin C content are very high. These nutrients are classified as antioxidants and are thought to protect against damage to body tissues and thereby help ward off diseases.

Per Serving: Calories 89; Total Fat 5 g; Saturated Fat 1 g; Cholesterol 0 mg; Sodium 511 mg; Carbohydrate 9 g; Fiber 3 g; Protein 3 g; Calcium 108 mg

Tangy Turnips and Spinach

Makes 4 servings

1¹/₂ pounds turnips, peeled, chopped into ³/₄-inch pieces
2 garlic cloves, minced
1 tablespoon red pepper flakes
1 tablespoon olive oil
1 pound spinach, trimmed, chopped
1 tablespoon vinegar
Salt and pepper to taste

Method of preparation

▼ Combine the turnips with enough water to cover in a saucepan. Simmer for 30 to 35 minutes or until the turnips are tender; drain.
▼ Sauté the garlic and red pepper flakes in the olive oil in a saucepan over medium heat for 1 minute. Add the spinach and vinegar and mix well.
▼ Steam, covered, for 3 to 4 minutes or until the spinach wilts. Stir in the turnips, salt and pepper.
▼ Cook just until heated through, stirring occasionally.

The turnip is known for its nutritious greens and distinctive-tasting root. Historically, turnips have been thought of as peasant food. Another underused yet nutritious vegetable, turnips often are seen only on the Thanksgiving Day table, even though they are in peak season from October to March.

Per Serving: Calories 104; Total Fat 4 g; Saturated Fat 1 g; Cholesterol 0 mg; Sodium 204 mg; Carbohydrate 15 g; Fiber 6 g; Protein 5 g; Calcium 167 mg

Spicy Stir-Fried Vegetables

Makes 4 servings

1 teaspoon peanut oil
4 ounces tofu, cut into $1/2$-inch pieces
$1/2$ cup ($1/2$-inch pieces) onion
3 garlic cloves, minced
1 teaspoon minced gingerroot
1 cup chopped bok choy
1 cup ($1/2$-inch pieces) zucchini
$1/2$ cup ($1/2$-inch pieces) carrot
$1/2$ cup canned chopped tomatoes
2 tablespoons peanut butter
2 tablespoons lime juice
1 tablespoon chopped fresh cilantro

Method of preparation

▼ Heat the peanut oil in a nonstick skillet until hot. Add the tofu. Stir-fry until brown. Remove the tofu to a paper towel to drain.
▼ Stir-fry the onion, garlic and gingerroot in the same skillet over medium heat for 5 minutes or until tender. Add the bok choy, zucchini and carrot and mix well.
▼ Stir-fry for 5 to 6 minutes. Stir in the tomatoes, peanut butter and lime juice.
▼ Simmer, covered, for 10 minutes, stirring occasionally. Add the tofu and cilantro and mix gently.
▼ Spoon onto a heated serving platter. Serve immediately.

Many vegetarians rely on tofu for its high protein content and versatility. But you don't have to be a vegetarian to enjoy tofu; you just need to know what to do with it! The simplest way to prepare tofu is to stir-fry it as illustrated in this recipe. Essential to working with tofu is using highly flavored ingredients for seasoning and handling the tofu gently.

Per Serving: Calories 101; Total Fat 6 g; Saturated Fat 1 g; Cholesterol 0 mg; Sodium 135 mg;
Carbohydrate 9 g; Fiber 2 g; Protein 5 g; Calcium 70 mg

Honey-Glazed Plantains

Makes 4 servings

4 plantains
1/2 cup light sour cream
2 tablespoons honey
1 tablespoon melted butter
1/4 teaspoon cinnamon
1/8 teaspoon allspice

Method of preparation

▼ Preheat the oven to 350 degrees.
▼ Cut the plantains into halves; do not peel. Combine with enough water to cover in a saucepan. Bring to a boil; reduce heat.
▼ Cook for 10 minutes or until tender. Pierce the plantains with the tip of a knife. Remove from the water; peel.
▼ Process the plantains, sour cream, honey, butter, cinnamon and allspice in a food processor until puréed. Spoon into a baking dish.
▼ Bake for 10 minutes or until hot.

Delectable enough to be dessert, though most often served as a side dish. Botanically a fruit, plantains are often referred to as a vegetable because they are starchy and must be cooked before eating. The amount of potassium in plantains is almost double that of regular bananas. This mineral aids the fluid balance in body cells, assists in muscle contractions, and is important for energy metabolism.

Per Serving: Calories 204; Total Fat 4 g; Saturated Fat 2 g; Cholesterol 10 mg; Sodium 41 mg; Carbohydrate 45 g; Fiber 3 g; Protein 2 g; Calcium 7 mg

Sweetness and excitement do not have to disappear
when you are changing your dessert-eating paradigm.
Only fat and calories need fall by the wayside!

Dessert goes beyond cakes, pies, and cookies.
The preparation of the recipes offered here focuses on the use
of high-quality ingredients, especially ripe fruits
and versatile dairy products. Satisfy your sweet tooth with
Fresh Peach Crisp, Strawberry Yogurt Mousse with Grand Marnier
Sauce, or an Iced Berry Compote.

Often dessert is considered nothing more than
a sugary concoction that offers a sweet fix but relatively
nothing more than calories. Not here . . . vitamins,
minerals, and fiber can be found in these selections and
the best part is that no one will ever guess!

No matter what kind of dessert you choose,
the key to having it within the context of a healthy diet is
truly **moderation**. Choose dessert when you really
know you will enjoy it. Also watch the amount you eat, as
the old saying of "It's not what you eat, it's how much"
has a strong ring of truth.

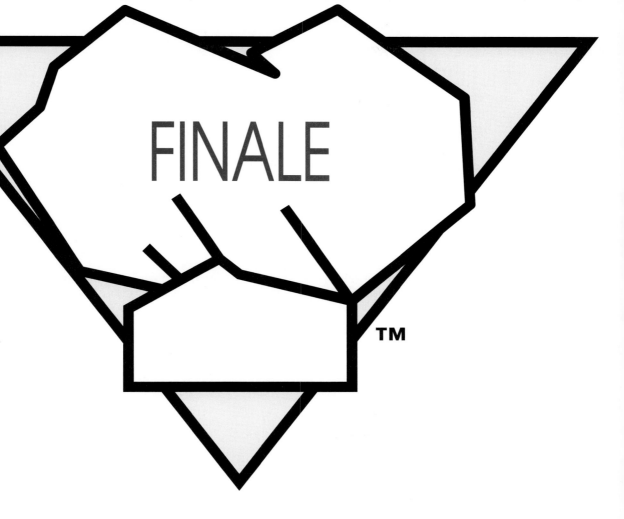

FINALE

™

DESSERTS

Iced Berry Compote

Makes 4 servings

1/2 cup sugar
1/4 cup water
1 tablespoon lemon juice
1 cup blueberries
1 cup blackberries
1 cup strawberries
2 pints frozen vanilla fat-free yogurt

Method of preparation
▼ Combine the sugar, water and lemon juice in a bowl and mix well. Add the blueberries, blackberries and strawberries and mix gently.
▼ Chill for 45 minutes before serving.
▼ Place 2 scoops of the yogurt in each of 4 wine glasses. Top with the berry compote. Serve immediately.

A large, purplish-black, and glossy fruit, blackberries are not always easy to find due to their extreme perishability and short growing season. Try loganberries or raspberries, if available. Better yet, start a bush in a remote corner of your yard and you will have ready access to this luscious fruit every year.

Per Serving: Calories 238; Total Fat 0 g; Saturated Fat 0 g; Cholesterol 0 mg; Sodium 68 mg; Carbohydrate 56 g; Fiber 4 g; Protein 5 g; Calcium 100 mg

Blueberry and Strawberry Crème Brûlée

Makes 4 servings

2¹/₂ cups sliced strawberries
1 cup blueberries
1 tablespoon Grand Marnier
1 cup light sour cream
Cinnamon to taste
¹/₄ cup packed brown sugar

Method of preparation

▼ Combine the strawberries, blueberries and Grand Marnier in a bowl and mix gently.
  Chill for 20 minutes.
▼ Preheat the broiler.
▼ Spoon the berry mixture into 4 ovenproof dessert dishes. Spread with a mixture of the
  sour cream and cinnamon. Sprinkle with the brown sugar.
▼ Broil 4 inches from the heat source for 15 to 20 seconds or until the brown sugar melts
  slightly.
▼ Let stand for 3 minutes before serving.

If you find yourself in Maine or Minnesota during the summer months, treat yourself to this confection made with the tiny tart-sweet wild blueberry. The rest of us will make do with the larger cultivated berries, which are more widely available. Like most fruits these berries are a good source of vitamins A and C and fiber. Blueberries will stay fresh in the refrigerator in their original container for approximately one week.

Per Serving: Calories 116; Total Fat 2 g; Saturated Fat 0 g; Cholesterol 5 mg; Sodium 21 mg;
Carbohydrate 23 g; Fiber 3 g; Protein 2 g; Calcium 23 mg

Figs with Honey and Raspberry Cream

Makes 4 servings

12 fresh figs, sliced into quarters
1 tablespoon rum
1 cup light sour cream
$^1/_2$ cup raspberries, mashed
2 tablespoons honey

Method of preparation
▼ Combine the figs and rum in a bowl and mix gently.
▼ Chill for 20 minutes. Spoon into 4 wine glasses.
▼ Combine the sour cream, raspberries and honey in a bowl and mix well. Pour over the figs.
▼ Serve immediately.

Break the paradigm of empty-calorie desserts. This recipe provides six grams of fiber per serving, almost unheard of in a meal, let alone a dessert. Fresh figs are widely available from June to mid-November. Use your nose in the selection process. Figs should smell sweet, not sour.

Per Serving: Calories 179; Total Fat 2 g; Saturated Fat 0 g; Cholesterol 5 mg; Sodium 16 mg; Carbohydrate 40 g; Fiber 6 g; Protein 2 g; Calcium 57 mg

Fresh Peach Crisp

Makes 4 servings

2 cups sliced peeled fresh peaches
1 tablespoon lime juice
1 tablespoon brandy
1 teaspoon cinnamon
$1/8$ teaspoon nutmeg
$1/2$ cup rolled oats
$1/4$ cup packed brown sugar
2 tablespoons melted margarine

Method of preparation

▼ Preheat the oven to 350 degrees.
▼ Combine the peaches, lime juice, brandy, cinnamon and nutmeg in a bowl and mix well. Spoon into a baking dish sprayed with nonstick cooking spray.
▼ Combine the oats, brown sugar and margarine in a bowl and mix well. Sprinkle over the prepared layer.
▼ Bake for 35 minutes or until brown and bubbly.
▼ Cool slightly before serving.

Originating in China, peaches were considered a symbol of immortality to the ancient Chinese. A good source of vitamin A and potassium, fresh peaches are available in the summer. Purchase ripe peaches for the best flavor, as peaches do not ripen properly once they are picked.

Per Serving: Calories 172; Total Fat 6 g; Saturated Fat 1 g; Cholesterol 0 mg; Sodium 71 mg;
Carbohydrate 26 g; Fiber 3 g; Protein 2 g; Calcium 27 mg

Golden Delicious Apple Crisp

Makes 4 servings

4 cups ($1/2$-inch slices) peeled Golden Delicious apples
$1/3$ cup orange juice
$1/4$ cup sugar
1 cup rolled oats
$1/2$ cup packed brown sugar
2 tablespoons melted margarine
$3/4$ teaspoon cinnamon
$1/2$ teaspoon nutmeg

Method of preparation
▼ Preheat the oven to 350 degrees.
▼ Combine the apples, orange juice and sugar in a bowl and mix well. Spoon into a baking dish sprayed with nonstick cooking spray.
▼ Combine the oats, brown sugar, margarine, cinnamon and nutmeg in a bowl and mix well. Sprinkle over the apple mixture.
▼ Bake for 25 to 30 minutes or until the top is golden brown and the apples are tender.
▼ Cool slightly before serving.

Traditional apple crisp weighs in at double the fat and saturated fat of this lighter, yet still savory, treat. Another plus is that apples and oats contain soluble fiber. This type of fiber can bind cholesterol compounds and carry them out of the body, thus helping to decrease your blood cholesterol level.

Per Serving: Calories 319; Total Fat 7 g; Saturated Fat 1 g; Cholesterol 0 mg; Sodium 279 mg; Carbohydrate 63 g; Fiber 6 g; Protein 4 g; Calcium 150 mg

Dutch Cocoa Mousse

Makes 4 servings

1/3 cup sugar
1/4 cup baking cocoa
2 1/2 tablespoons cornstarch
1 3/4 cups skim milk
1 egg, slightly beaten
1/2 teaspoon vanilla extract
1/4 cup whipping cream

Method of preparation

▼ Combine the sugar, baking cocoa and cornstarch in a saucepan and mix well. Stir in the skim milk.
▼ Cook over medium heat until thickened, whisking constantly. Remove from heat. Stir a small amount of the hot mixture into the egg; stir the egg into the hot mixture.
▼ Add the vanilla, whisking constantly for 1 minute. Cool in an ice bath.
▼ Beat the whipping cream in a mixer bowl at high speed until stiff peaks form. Add the cocoa mixture gradually, beating constantly until light and fluffy.
▼ Spoon into 4 champagne glasses. Serve immediately.

Need a chocolate fix? This mousse, lower in fat, cholesterol, and calories than the traditional version, will fool the scale but not your palate. Cocoa powder is defatted chocolate. When chocolate is processed into cocoa, the unmatched taste of chocolate is left behind but not the fat and its calories. For an elegant presentation, top each serving with whipped cream and sprinkle with chocolate shavings.

Per Serving: Calories 200; Total Fat 8 g; Saturated Fat 4 g; Cholesterol 75 mg; Sodium 78 mg; Carbohydrate 29 g; Fiber 2 g; Protein 7 g; Calcium 155 mg

Strawberry Yogurt Mousse with Grand Marnier Sauce

Makes 4 servings

For the mousse

1 tablespoon unflavored gelatin
3/4 cup cold orange juice
1/3 cup sugar
1 1/2 cups sliced strawberries
1 cup strawberry low-fat yogurt
1/4 cup whipping cream
1/2 cup sliced strawberries

For the sauce

1 cup orange juice
1/4 cup orange marmalade
3 tablespoons Grand Marnier
2 tablespoons chopped fresh mint

To prepare the mousse

▼ Soften the gelatin in the cold orange juice in a bowl and mix well. Combine the gelatin mixture and sugar in a saucepan.
▼ Cook over low heat until the gelatin dissolves, stirring constantly.
▼ Process 1 1/2 cups strawberries in a food processor until puréed. Stir into the gelatin mixture. Add the yogurt, whisking until blended.
▼ Beat the whipping cream in a bowl with a wire whisk until stiff peaks form. Fold into the gelatin mixture with a rubber spatula. Spoon into four 6-ounce soufflé dishes. Chill for 3 hours or until set.

To prepare the sauce

▼ Combine the orange juice, orange marmalade and Grand Marnier in a saucepan. Bring to a boil; reduce heat.
▼ Simmer until reduced by 1/2, stirring constantly. Cool to room temperature. Stir in the mint.

To assemble

▼ Set the soufflé dishes in a pan of hot water. Let stand until the edges pull from the sides of the dishes. Invert onto 4 dessert plates.
▼ Overlap the remaining strawberry slices on the top of each mousse; drizzle with the sauce. Serve immediately.

The mere thought of a fresh, warm, ripe strawberry sets one's mouth watering. Containing fifty-five calories, a cup of the red berries abounds in vitamin C and contains a fair amount of potassium. Choose berries carefully, looking for those that are brightly colored, firm, and have hulls attached. Unlike many fruits, strawberries do not ripen after they are picked. Refrigerate strawberries after purchase, and use within a day or two. A pint yields about 2 cups of sliced berries.

Per Serving: Calories 336; Total Fat 7 g; Saturated Fat 4 g; Cholesterol 23 mg; Sodium 50 mg; Carbohydrate 62 g; Fiber 2 g; Protein 4 g; Calcium 120 mg

Grand Marnier Caramel Cream

Makes 4 servings

3 eggs
1 1/2 cups skim milk
1/4 cup sugar
3 tablespoons nonfat dry milk
2 tablespoons Grand Marnier
1/2 teaspoon grated orange zest
2 tablespoons sugar

Method of preparation

▼ Preheat the oven to 350 degrees.
▼ Beat the eggs in a mixer bowl. Add the skim milk, 1/4 cup sugar, dry milk powder and Grand Marnier and beat until blended. Stir in the orange zest.
▼ Heat 2 tablespoons sugar in a saucepan over medium heat until the sugar starts to melt and turns brown, stirring constantly. Remove from heat.
▼ Spray four 6-ounce ovenproof baking dishes with nonstick cooking spray. Pour just enough of the brown sugar syrup into each dish to cover the bottom. Top with the Grand Marnier mixture.
▼ Place the dishes in a shallow pan; add hot water to a depth of 1 inch.
▼ Bake for 35 minutes. Remove the dishes from the hot water. Let stand for 30 minutes.
▼ Run a sharp knife around the edges of the baking dishes to loosen. Invert onto individual dessert dishes. Serve immediately.

Sweet-sounding caramel is no more than browned sugar, although it does have a marvelous flavor. Using synthetic or artificial sweeteners in place of the sugar is not recommended, since their texture and sweetening ability are adversely affected by heat. We prefer to use a little of the "real stuff."

Per Serving: Calories 199; Total Fat 4 g; Saturated Fat 1 g; Cholesterol 162 mg; Sodium 112 mg; Carbohydrate 28 g; Fiber 0 g; Protein 9 g; Calcium 172 mg

Lime Sponge Pudding

Makes 4 servings

1 cup 1% milk
2/3 cup sugar
1/4 cup lime juice
2 egg yolks
3 tablespoons flour
1 teaspoon grated lime peel
2 egg whites

Method of preparation
▼ Preheat the oven to 325 degrees.
▼ Combine the milk, sugar, lime juice, egg yolks, flour and lime peel in a bowl and mix well.
▼ Beat the egg whites in a mixer bowl until stiff peaks form. Fold into the lime mixture. Spoon into a 1-quart baking dish.
▼ Place the baking dish in a shallow baking pan; add water to a depth of 1 inch.
▼ Bake for 50 to 55 minutes. Let stand for 15 minutes before serving.

"Limeys" is the nickname for British seamen who were fed lime and other citrus juices to prevent scurvy. As a result, the lime has gained notoriety as a rich and tasty source of vitamin C. When using lime juice, fresh is the best. To get the greatest amount of juice out of the fruit, roll the lime on a hard surface while gently but firmly pressing with the palm of your hand.

Per Serving: Calories 218; Total Fat 3 g; Saturated Fat 1 g; Cholesterol 109 mg; Sodium 62 mg; Carbohydrate 42 g; Fiber 0 g; Protein 6 g; Calcium 91 mg

Summer Pudding

Makes 4 servings

2 cups sliced strawberries
1 cup blueberries
1 cup raspberries
1 cup chopped peeled Granny Smith apple
$1/2$ cup seedless grape halves
$1/3$ cup sugar
5 slices white bread, crusts trimmed, torn into pieces

Method of preparation

▼ Combine the strawberries, blueberries, raspberries, apple, grapes and sugar in a bowl and mix gently.
▼ Let stand at room temperature for 1 hour. Drain, reserving the juices.
▼ Line the bottom and side of a bowl with 3 of the torn bread pieces. Drizzle with $1/2$ of the reserved juices.
▼ Spoon the fruit into the bowl. Top with the remaining bread pieces; drizzle with the remaining reserved juices. Cover with plastic wrap; press lightly.
▼ Chill for 8 to 10 hours. Invert onto a serving platter.
▼ Cut into 4 wedges. Place on chilled dessert plates. Serve immediately.

Turn bread into bounty! Simple ingredients make this dessert a perfect summer offering. The added sugar is kept to a minimum since fresh ripe fruit contributes natural sugars to the fruit juices. This unique dessert is at its best when allowed to set overnight and served with crème anglaise.

Per Serving: Calories 230; Total Fat 2 g; Saturated Fat 0 g; Cholesterol 0 mg; Sodium 174 mg; Carbohydrate 52 g; Fiber 6 g; Protein 4 g; Calcium 57 mg

Sweet Potato Pudding

Makes 4 serving

1 cup chopped sweet potatoes
1/2 cup orange juice
1/4 cup packed brown sugar
2 egg yolks
1 tablespoon melted margarine
1/4 teaspoon ground cloves
1/4 teaspoon cinnamon
1/4 teaspoon nutmeg
2 egg whites
1 tablespoon sugar

Method of preparation

▼ Preheat the oven to 325 degrees.
▼ Combine the sweet potatoes with enough water to cover in a saucepan. Bring to a boil; reduce heat.
▼ Simmer for 25 to 30 minutes or until tender; drain.
▼ Mash the sweet potatoes in a bowl until smooth. Add the orange juice, brown sugar, egg yolks, margarine, cloves, cinnamon and nutmeg and mix well.
▼ Beat the egg whites in a bowl with a wire whisk until soft peaks form. Add the sugar. Beat until stiff peaks form. Fold into the sweet potato mixture. Spoon into a 1-quart baking dish sprayed with nonstick cooking spray.
▼ Place the baking dish in a shallow baking pan; add water to a depth of 1 inch.
▼ Bake for 1 hour. Let stand for 5 minutes before serving.

A vegetable for dessert? Yes, yes, yes! Deep-orange sweet potatoes make for an extraordinary vitamin A-rich sweet meal ending. Sweet potatoes are often confused with yams. The yam is dry and firm, while the sweet potato has a moist, soft flesh. The yam hails from the North, while sweet potatoes are grown in the southern states.

Per Serving: Calories 159; Total Fat 6 g; Saturated Fat 1 g; Cholesterol 106 mg; Sodium 73 mg; Carbohydrate 24 g; Fiber 1 g; Protein 4 g; Calcium 35 mg

Yogurt Rice Pudding with Dried Fruits

Makes 4 servings

^{1}/2 cup sugar
2 eggs, beaten
1 teaspoon vanilla extract
1^1/4 cups cooked rice
1 cup low-fat lemon yogurt
^{3}/4 cup chopped dried mixed fruit
^{2}/3 cup skim milk

Method of preparation

▼ Preheat the oven to 350 degrees.
▼ Combine the sugar, eggs and vanilla in a bowl, whisking until pale yellow. Add the rice, yogurt, mixed fruit and skim milk and mix well.
▼ Spoon into a 1-quart baking dish. Place the dish in a shallow baking pan; add hot water to a depth of 1 inch.
▼ Bake for 1 hour. Cool for 1 hour before serving.

Dried fruits are concentrated packages of nutrients including fiber and iron. Most dried fruits are available all year long and can be kept for months without refrigeration. They are also good sources of sugar and calories, so a little goes a long way.

Per Serving: Calories 328; Total Fat 4 g; Saturated Fat 1 g; Cholesterol 110 mg; Sodium 95 mg; Carbohydrate 66 g; Fiber 0 g; Protein 10 g; Calcium 175 mg

Low-Fat Cinnamon Crème Anglaise

Makes 8 servings

1 cup skim milk
2 tablespoons sugar
1 tablespoon cornstarch
1 small egg yolk, beaten
$1/2$ teaspoon vanilla extract
$1/8$ teaspoon cinnamon

Method of preparation
▼ Combine the skim milk, sugar and cornstarch in a saucepan and mix well.
▼ Bring to a boil over medium heat, whisking constantly. Remove from heat. Stir a small amount of the hot mixture into the egg yolk; stir the egg yolk into the hot mixture. Add the vanilla and cinnamon and mix well.
▼ Let stand until cool. Chill, covered, until serving time.
▼ Serve with fresh fruit.

Cholesterol savings abound in this version of Low-Fat Cinnamon Crème Anglaise, which utilizes fewer than half the egg yolks of the traditional version. No guest will ever know since the finished product is still creamy and delicious. Perfect as a topping for fresh summer berries.

Per 2-Tablespoon Serving: Calories 34; Total Fat 1 g; Saturated Fat 0 g; Cholesterol 27 mg; Sodium 17 mg; Carbohydrate 6 g; Fiber 0 g; Protein 1 g; Calcium 41 mg

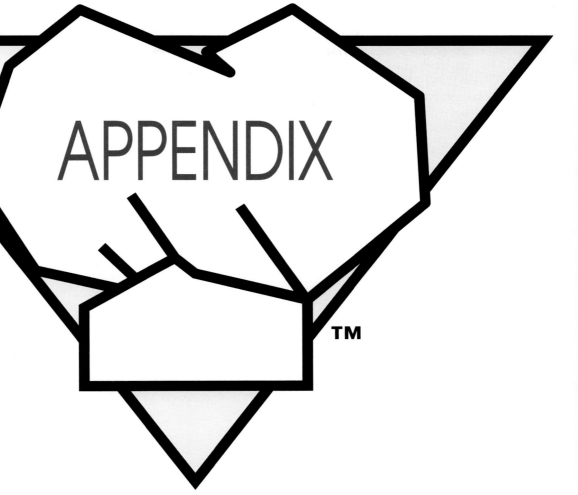

TASTEFUL SHIFT IN HEALTHY EATING

APPENDIX

™

Asian Plum Sauce

Makes 6 servings

1 cup chopped peeled apple
1 cup chopped plums
1 cup chopped apricots
1/2 cup rice vinegar
1/4 cup honey
2 tablespoons soy sauce
1 teaspoon ground ginger

Method of preparation
▼ Combine the apple, plums, apricots, rice vinegar, honey, soy sauce and ginger in a saucepan and mix well.
▼ Simmer until the fruits are tender, stirring occasionally.
▼ Press the fruits with a plastic spatula through a strainer into a bowl. Return the purée to the saucepan.
▼ Simmer until slightly thickened, stirring constantly.
▼ Chill, covered, in the refrigerator until serving time.

A traditional condiment for Asian dishes, this plum sauce is best when made with fresh ripe fruits. For variety, add a small amount of additional vinegar and use as a marinade. Although nonfat, use with good judgment, as the calories can add up quickly.

Per 1/4-Cup Serving: Calories 88; Total Fat 0 g; Saturated Fat 0 g; Cholesterol 0 mg; Sodium 277 mg; Carbohydrate 23 g; Fiber 2 g; Protein 1 g; Calcium 9 mg

Oriental Spicy Sauce

Makes 6 servings

6 tablespoons soy sauce
3 tablespoons sake
3 tablespoons rice vinegar
3 tablespoons chopped scallions
2 tablespoons grated gingerroot
2 tablespoons sugar
1 tablespoon chili paste

Method of preparation

▼ Combine the soy sauce, sake and rice vinegar in a saucepan and mix well. Bring to a boil over medium heat; reduce heat.
▼ Simmer for 10 minutes, stirring occasionally. Stir in the scallions, gingerroot, sugar and chili paste.
▼ Simmer for 5 minutes, stirring occasionally.
▼ Chill, covered, until serving time. May store in the refrigerator for up to 2 weeks.

A very light, mildly hot, and versatile sauce. Those who prefer the spicier side of life can simply add more chili paste. Practically void of fat, this sauce can be used liberally by all but sodium watchers. A real pick-me-up to unadorned Oriental noodles or rice.

Per 1/4-Cup Serving: Calories 41; Total Fat 0 g; Saturated Fat 0 g; Cholesterol 0 mg; Sodium 916 mg; Carbohydrate 7 g; Fiber 0 g; Protein 1 g; Calcium 9 mg

Spicy Sweet Enchilada Sauce

Makes 5 servings

3/4 cup (1/8-inch pieces) red onion
1 garlic clove, minced
1 teaspoon olive oil
2 tablespoons chili powder
1/2 teaspoon cumin
1/2 teaspoon oregano
2 cups chunky tomato sauce
2 tablespoons brown sugar
1/4 teaspoon cayenne

Method of preparation

▼ Sauté the red onion and garlic in the olive oil in a saucepan over medium heat for 2 to 3 minutes. Stir in the chili powder, cumin and oregano.
▼ Sauté for 5 minutes. Add the tomato sauce, brown sugar and cayenne and mix well. Bring to a boil, stirring frequently. Remove from heat.
▼ Let stand until cool.

It's true! The secret usually is in the sauce, and this recipe is no exception. These spicy and sweet ingredients blend together in a magical way. The result . . . a sauce with minimal fat and salt that everyone who encounters is bound to like.

Per 1/2-Cup Serving: Calories 74; Total Fat 2 g; Saturated Fat 0 g; Cholesterol 0 mg; Sodium 48 mg; Carbohydrate 15 g; Fiber 2 g; Protein 2 g; Calcium 31 mg

Tangy Yogurt Sauce

Makes 5 servings

1 teaspoon cumin seeds
$1/2$ teaspoon cardamom
$1/2$ teaspoon fennel seeds
$1/8$ teaspoon turmeric
1 tablespoon olive oil
1 cup plain nonfat yogurt
2 garlic cloves, chopped
2 tablespoons minced fresh cilantro
1 teaspoon lime juice
1 teaspoon minced gingerroot
Salt and pepper to taste

Method of preparation

▼ Sauté the cumin seeds, cardamom, fennel seeds and turmeric in the olive oil in a saucepan over medium heat for 5 minutes. Crush the herbs with a flat-bottom pan.
▼ Combine the yogurt, garlic, cilantro, lime juice, gingerroot, salt and pepper in a bowl and mix well. Stir in the sautéed herbs.
▼ Chill, covered, for 15 minutes before serving.

One of the most versatile food products of all time . . . yogurt! Put on your paradigm-busting hat and invent ways to savor this tangy delight. Drizzle over a mixed greens salad, cooked vegetables, or add to a cold bean salad. This is an easy way to boost your calcium intake regardless of your preference.

Per $1/4$-Cup Serving: Calories 58; Total Fat 3 g; Saturated Fat 0 g; Cholesterol 1 mg; Sodium 38 mg; Carbohydrate 5 g; Fiber 0 g; Protein 3 g; Calcium 109 mg

Roasted Red Pepper and Tomato Coulis

Makes 7 servings

4 red bell peppers
8 red tomatoes
1 1/2 cups chicken stock
1 tablespoon olive oil
1 tablespoon balsamic vinegar
1 tablespoon chopped fresh basil
1 teaspoon sugar
3 garlic cloves, sliced

Method of preparation

▼ Preheat the oven to 450 degrees.
▼ Place the red peppers on a baking sheet.
▼ Roast for 10 minutes. Place the tomatoes on the baking sheet.
▼ Roast for 10 minutes longer or until the tomato skins begin to brown and blister and the bell peppers are brown. Place the bell peppers in a sealable plastic bag.
▼ Steam for 20 minutes or until cool. Peel and seed the bell peppers, discarding the skins and seeds.
▼ Combine the bell peppers, tomatoes, stock, olive oil, balsamic vinegar, basil, sugar and garlic in a food processor container. Process until puréed.
▼ Spoon the purée into a saucepan. Bring to a boil, stirring frequently; reduce heat.
▼ Simmer until slightly thickened, stirring constantly. Serve warm.

A coulis is a purée of vegetables used to flavor dishes. Red bell peppers make for a wonderful coulis ingredient. If in a rush, roasted red peppers are available in most supermarkets or gourmet stores. Coulis may also be used to decorate the plate on which your meat, poultry, or fish is being served.

Per 1/4-Cup Serving: Calories 66; Total Fat 3 g; Saturated Fat 0 g; Cholesterol 0 mg; Sodium 14 mg; Carbohydrate 11 g; Fiber 3 g; Protein 2 g; Calcium 27 mg

Sweet Corn and Chile Pepper Relish

Makes 6 servings

3 ears corn, roasted
2 anaheim peppers, chopped
2 jalapeños, chopped
1 cup chopped seeded cucumber
$1/4$ cup chopped red onion
$1/4$ cup chopped scallions
$1/4$ cup chopped red bell pepper
$1/4$ cup chopped green bell pepper
$1/4$ cup lime juice
1 tablespoon olive oil
1 teaspoon chili powder
1 teaspoon sugar
$1/2$ teaspoon cumin
Salt and pepper to taste

Method of preparation
▼ Scrape the corn kernels with a sharp knife into a bowl. Stir in the anaheim peppers, jalapeños, cucumber, red onion, scallions, bell peppers, lime juice, olive oil, chili powder, sugar, cumin, salt and pepper.
▼ Chill, covered, in the refrigerator for 2 hours before serving.

A relish can perk up the presentation of any dish. The anaheim and jalapeño peppers will perk up your tastebuds as well. Substitute with your favorite chile pepper or omit if your prefer. Either way, a small $1/4$-cup serving provides 2 grams of fiber, the same amount found in a slice of whole wheat bread.

Per $1/4$-Cup Serving: Calories 74; Total Fat 3 g; Saturated Fat 0 g; Cholesterol 0 mg; Sodium 13 mg; Carbohydrate 12 g; Fiber 2 g; Protein 2 g; Calcium 13 mg

Chicken Stock
Makes 1¹/2 quarts

6 chicken legs
2 quarts water
¹/2 cup chopped onion
1 leek, chopped
1 carrot, chopped
1 rib celery, chopped
1 teaspoon crushed gingerroot
1 teaspoon thyme
1 teaspoon rosemary

Method of preparation
▼ Rinse the chicken.
▼ Combine the chicken, water, onion, leek, carrot, celery, gingerroot, thyme and rosemary in a stockpot. Bring to a boil over medium heat; reduce heat. Remove any residue that floats to the top with a spoon and discard.
▼ Simmer for 2¹/2 hours. Strain through cheesecloth or a strainer into a bowl, discarding the chicken and vegetables.
▼ Chill, covered, for 8 to 10 hours. Skim the top before using.

An absolute staple in any great cook's kitchen is homemade chicken stock! Seasonings can be varied to your taste. Just remember to make a lot. Freeze extra stock in ice cube trays and store in food storage bags in the freezer for months. Cubes can be used to minimize the use of oil when steaming vegetables or when sautéing.

Per Serving: Calories 39; Total Fat 1 g; Sodium 26 mg

Vegetable Stock

Makes 1¹/₂ quarts

2 quarts water
1 cup thinly sliced celery
1 cup chopped turnip
1 cup sliced peeled carrot
1 cup chopped onion
1 cup chopped mushrooms
4 leeks, chopped
¹/₂ cup white wine
¹/₄ cup chopped fresh parsley
¹/₄ cup chopped fresh basil
8 garlic cloves, chopped
4 teaspoons rosemary
4 teaspoons thyme

Method of preparation
▼ Combine the water, celery, turnip, carrot, onion, mushrooms, leeks, white wine, parsley, basil, garlic, rosemary and thyme in a stockpot and mix well. Bring to a boil gradually; reduce heat. Remove any residue that floats to the top and discard.
▼ Simmer for 1¹/₂ hours; discard the vegetables. Strain the stock through cheesecloth or a strainer into a bowl.
▼ Let stand until cool. Chill, covered, for 8 to 10 hours.

Not as popular as chicken stock, but certainly as handy. If you prefer, substitute root vegetables native to your locale or which are to your liking. Bundle herbs into a tightly tied cheesecloth sack, and you have created a bouquet garni, or simply leave herbs loose as described and strain before serving.

Per Serving: Calories 28; Total Fat 0 g; Sodium 13 mg

Sweet Blackberry Ginger Vinegar

Makes 10 servings

2 cups rice vinegar
1/2 cup blackberries
1/2 cup sugar
1 tablespoon minced gingerroot

Method of preparation

▼ Combine the rice vinegar, blackberries, sugar and gingerroot in a food processor container.
▼ Process until puréed. Spoon into a glass bowl.
▼ Chill, covered, for 3 days. Strain, discarding any solids.
▼ Bottle the vinegar. Store in the refrigerator.

Once you've made and enjoyed a flavored vinegar, you'll never want to go back to the unflavored. Use this vinegar as a substitute in homemade salad dressings or for cooking vegetables, as illustrated in Braised Swiss Chard (see page 138). Flavored vinegars make for interesting marinades as well.

Per 1/4-Cup Serving: Calories 50; Total Fat 0 g; Saturated Fat 0 g; Cholesterol 0 mg; Sodium 1 mg; Carbohydrate 14 g; Fiber 0 g; Protein 0 g; Calcium 5 mg

Wine Pronunciation Guide

Semidry White Wine

These wines have a fresh fruity taste and are best served young and slightly chilled.

▼ Johannisberg Riesling – (*Yo-hann-is-burg Rees-ling*)
▼ Frascati – (*Fras-cah-tee*)
▼ Gewürztraminer – (*Ge-vert-tram-me-ner*)
▼ Bernkasteler – (*Barn-kahst-ler*)

▼ Sylvaner Riesling – (*Sil-vah-nur Rees-ling*)
▼ Est! Est! Est!
▼ Fendant – (*Fahn-dawn*)
▼ Dienheimer – (*Deen-heim-er*)
▼ Krauznacher – (*Kroytz-nock*)

Dry White Wines

These wines have a crisp, refreshing taste and are best served young and slightly chilled.

▼ Vouvray – (*Voo-vray*)
▼ Chablis – (*Shab-lee*)
▼ Chardonnay – (*Shar-doh-nay*)
▼ Pinot Blanc – (*Pee-no Blawn*)
▼ Pouilly-Fuissé – (*Pwee-yee Fwee-say*)
▼ Orvieto Secco – (*Orv-yay-toe Sek-o*)
▼ Piesporter Trocken – (*Peez-porter*)

▼ Meursault – (*Mere-so*)
▼ Hermitage Blanc – (*Air-me-tahz Blawn*)
▼ Pinot Grigio – (*Pee-no Gree-jo*)
▼ Verdicchio – (*Ver-deek-ee-o*)
▼ Sancerre – (*Sahn-sehr*)
▼ Soave – (*So-ah-veh*)

Light Red Wines

These wines have a light taste and are best served young at cool room temperature.

▼ Beaujolais – (Bo-sho-lay)
▼ Bardolino – (*Bar-do-leen-o*)
▼ Valpolicella – (*Val-po-lee-chel-la*)
▼ Moulin-A-Vent Beaujolais – (*Moo-lon-ah-vahn*)
▼ Barbera – (*Bar-bear-ah*)
▼ Lambrusco – (*Lom-bruce-co*)
▼ Lirac – (*Lee-rack*)

▼ Nuits-Saint Georges "Villages" – (*Nwee San Zhorzh*)
▼ Gamay Beaujolais – (*Ga-mai Bo-sho-lay*)
▼ Santa Maddalena – (*Santa Mad-lay-nah*)
▼ Merlo di Ticino – (*Mair-lo dee Tee-chee-no*)

Hearty Red Wines

These wines have a heavier taste, improve with age, and are best opened thirty minutes before serving.

▼ Barbaresco – (*Bar-bah-rez-coe*)
▼ Barolo – (*Bah-ro-lo*)
▼ Zinfandel – (*Zin-fan-dell*)
▼ Chianti Riserva – (*Key-ahn-tee Ree-sairv-ah*)
▼ Cote Rotie – (*Coat Ro-tee*)
▼ Hermitage – (*Air-me-tahz*)
▼ Taurasi – (*Tah-rah-see*)

▼ Merlot – (*Mair-lo*)
▼ Syrah – (*Sir-rah*)
▼ Chateauneuf-Du-Pape – (*Shot-toe-nuff dew Pop*)
▼ Petite Sirah – (*Puh-teet Seer-rah*)
▼ Cote de Beaune – (*Coat duh Bone*)
▼ Cabernet Sauvignon – (*Cab-air-nay So-vin-yawn*)

Substitution Chart

Instead of	Use
1 teaspoon baking powder	$1/4$ teaspoon baking soda plus $1/2$ teaspoon cream of tartar
1 tablespoon cornstarch (for thickening)	2 tablespoons flour or 1 tablespoon tapioca
1 cup sifted all-purpose flour	1 cup plus 2 tablespoons sifted cake flour
1 cup dry bread crumbs	4 slices bread
1 cup buttermilk	1 cup sour milk or 1 cup yogurt
1 cup whipping cream	$3/4$ cup skim milk plus $1/3$ cup butter
1 cup light cream	$7/8$ cup skim milk plus 3 tablespoons butter
1 cup sour cream	$7/8$ cup sour milk plus 3 tablespoons butter
1 cup sour milk	1 cup milk plus 1 tablespoon vinegar or lemon juice, or 1 cup buttermilk
1 garlic clove	$1/8$ teaspoon garlic powder or $1/8$ teaspoon instant minced garlic or $3/4$ teaspoon garlic salt or 5 drops of liquid garlic
1 tablespoon minced gingerroot	$1/8$ teaspoon fresh powdered ginger
1 teaspoon lemon juice	$1/2$ teaspoon vinegar
1 tablespoon mustard	1 teaspoon dry mustard
1 medium onion	1 tablespoon dried minced onion or 1 teaspoon onion powder
8 ounces fresh mushrooms	6 ounces canned mushrooms, drained
1 (1-ounce) square chocolate	$1/4$ cup baking cocoa plus 1 teaspoon shortening
$1 2/3$ ounces semisweet chocolate	1 ounce unsweetened chocolate plus 4 teaspoons granulated sugar
1 cup honey	1 to $1 1/4$ cups sugar plus $1/4$ cup liquid, or 1 cup corn syrup or molasses
1 cup granulated sugar	1 cup packed brown sugar or 1 cup corn syrup, molasses or honey minus $1/4$ cup liquid

Food Guide Pyramid

A Guide to Daily Food Choices

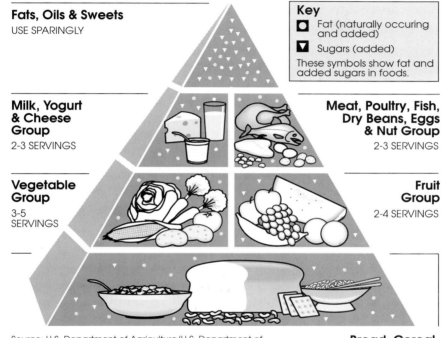

Fats, Oils & Sweets
USE SPARINGLY

Key
- ⬛ Fat (naturally occuring and added)
- ▼ Sugars (added)

These symbols show fat and added sugars in foods.

Milk, Yogurt & Cheese Group
2-3 SERVINGS

Meat, Poultry, Fish, Dry Beans, Eggs & Nut Group
2-3 SERVINGS

Vegetable Group
3-5 SERVINGS

Fruit Group
2-4 SERVINGS

Source: U.S. Department of Agriculture/U.S. Department of Health and Human Services

Bread, Cereal, Rice & Pasta Group
6-11 SERVINGS

Use the Food Guide Pyramid to help you eat better every day . . . the Dietary Guidelines way. Start with plenty of Breads, Cereals, Rice, and Pasta; Vegetables; and Fruits. Add two to three servings from the Milk group and two to three servings from the Meat group.

Each of these food groups provides some, but not all, of the nutrients you need. No one food group is more important than another—for good health you need them all. Go easy on fats, oils, and sweets—the foods in the small tip of the Pyramid.

Nutritional Profile Guidelines

The editors have attempted to present these recipes in a form that allows approximate nutritional values to be computed. Persons with dietary or health problems or whose diets require close monitoring should not rely solely on the nutritional information provided. They should consult their physicians or a registered dietitian for specific information.

Nutritional information for these recipes is computed from information derived from many sources, including materials supplied by the United States Department of Agriculture, computer databanks and journals in which the information is assumed to be in the public domain. However, many specialty items, new products and processed foods may not be available from these sources or may vary from the average values used in these profiles. More information on new and/or specific products may be obtained by reading the nutrient labels. Unless otherwise specified, the nutritional profile of these recipes is based on all measurements being level.

▼ **Alcoholic ingredients** have been analyzed for basic ingredients, although cooking causes the evaporation of alcohol, thus decreasing caloric content.

▼ **Eggs** are all large. To avoid raw eggs that may carry salmonella as in eggnog, use an equivalent amount of commercial egg substitute. There is less risk for salmonella if eggs are cooked.

▼ **Flour** is unsifted all-purpose flour.

▼ **Garnishes**, serving suggestions, and other optional additions and variations are not included in the profile.

▼ **Margarine** and **butter** are regular, not whipped, presoftened, or reduced-fat varieties.

▼ **Salt** and other ingredients to taste as noted in the ingredients have not been included in the nutritional profile.

Index

New Paradigm Cooking

Paradigm Cooking, Inc.
P.O. Box 3641
Cranston, Rhode Island 02910

Name _____

Address _____

City/State/Zip _____

Number of copies _____

Cost $18.95 per book _____

$3.50 postage and handling per book _____

(Rhode Island residents add $1.33 sales tax per book.) _____

Total Cost _____

Make checks payable to Paradigm Cooking, Inc.

New Paradigm Cooking

Paradigm Cooking, Inc.
P.O. Box 3641
Cranston, Rhode Island 02910

Name _____

Address _____

City/State/Zip _____

Number of copies _____

Cost $18.95 per book _____

$3.50 postage and handling per book _____

(Rhode Island residents add $1.33 sales tax per book.) _____

Total Cost _____

Make checks payable to Paradigm Cooking, Inc.